AF687124

It All Started with a Blog

Detangling the Wide Web of Disney Bloggers

Paul Lane

Theme Park Press
The Happiest Books on Earth
www.ThemeParkPress.com

Editor: Bob McLain
Layout: Artisanal Text

ISBN 979-8-89609-389-3
Printed in the United States of America

Theme Park Press | www.ThemeParkPress.com
Address queries to ben@themeparkpress.com

Contents

CHAPTER ONE

One Little Spark

The closest that mankind might every get to time travel is the acreage of amusement that constitute the parks owned and operated by the Walt Disney Company. Not the literal, flux capacitor-fueled type of time travel, mind you. But the sort of metaphorical time travel where one can almost literally live like a child again, if only for a few days (minus, you know, the need to raise thousands of dollars).

When a person is visiting one of the Disney Parks, one can allow him or herself to largely forget about time, work, school, annoying neighbors who drag race down the street all night and pretty much the world at large. Constraints and annoyances still exist while attending a Disney park, mind you, but they exist within the strict confines of Main Street parades, Fantasmic performances and bridges that take you from England to France in 30 seconds. The parks are surrounded by a force field of sorts—almost like Wakanda, but rather than vibranium shields the advanced technology consists of data-storing wristbands and animated robotic humanoids named John that like to pick on their Uncle Orville.

This world is sheltered from the rest of the planet, existing solely for its visitors' benefit. It's where the good guys always win, and are easily defined. Within its domain, Dole Whip counts as a fruit, Aerosmith always has another super-stretch limo ready for its fans and an animatronic George Washington sitting next Grover Cleveland and Millard Fillmore is the most lyrically gifted version of the One-Dollar Founding Father ever to grace a stage.

Sure, you need to keep track of any reservations, and the eventual sunset will usher in such a sensational feeling of relief from the brutal sun that you're probably grinning right now as you read this and picture the sensation. Such realities are present only in a relative state, though. At Walt Disney World, Disneyland or any of the other parks, you can do as you please when you please and get lost in the world that's created—like, "forget whether you put pants on this morning" lost. This environment allows the visitor to straddle the fine mental line that separates electrified exhilaration from insanity. Kids can envelop themselves in the sort of magic that inspires them through a lifetime. And adults can travel back to a time when their biggest care was securing a seat on the half of the Jungle Cruise boat that gets more wet from the backside of water.

Who wouldn't want to experience that sort of feeling? What other place would compel sexagenarians to empty out their 401(k) accounts—with a gleeful grin, no less—to finance a three-generation jaunt with their grandkids?

Disney fanatics have known since the first time they meandered past the Dapper Dans and the Casey's Corner Pianist toward Cinderella's Castle or heard Walt Disney discuss his ever-expanding plans on "Wonderful World of Disney" that there was palpable joy about all things produced by the House of Mouse. They mailed away for Mickey Mouse Club fan club items, dutifully awaited the next edition of The Disney Magazine and recorded every episode of "Ducktales" on VHS (they probably also aced that old "Ducktales"

Nintendo video game, more than willingly blowing into the cartridge a dozen times to get it going).

Before web surfers got knocked off of AOL by their little brothers, ranked their first MySpace top eight or even realized the word "email" wasn't a typo, a lot of them sermonized about all things Disney. But it wasn't until the internet brought Disney fans together that many of them realized just how far-reaching this sentiment was. From Marcelline to Miami and Chicago to Colorado Springs, pockets of Disney fans occupied hours of their time checking out the latest and greatest the company had cooking. And they did it before most people could even begin to figure out how to share a video from computer to computer.

That meant that, for the most part, they reveled in swapping stories. There truly is nothing like your first time, and with a relative dearth of content in the internet's nascent years tales of virginal visits to Disneyland or Walt Disney World were among the biggest early draws. For the writers, it presented a chance to create a log of a once-in-a-lifetime moment to recall at will. For the consumers, it took them back to their first times and allowed them to share in the joy that the parks brought to another family. Anyone with a computer that could get on the internet could relive those first magical moments of their initial visit—or most recent trip—and recapture a theme park experience that no other company has ever been able to replicate. And they could do so instantly, which was an absolute novelty in a time when more homes got newspapers tossed onto their porches (a job known as "paperboy" used to carry out that task) than cable television wired into their living rooms.

"There's a passion that starts at the parks and travels through adulthood," said John Yaglenski, who was one of the first people to establish a Disney web content center with the Internet Community of Tomorrow, or InterCOT. "It's the experience. It's the feeling. And Disney does it so well—the sights, smells, touches, sounds. Everything comes together and hits all your senses. It leaves an impression. And then you come home and miss it. You start to think, 'How do I get back that feeling of being there?' People in the early days would read each other's trip reports endlessly just to get the feeling of being there. It's a passion that's sparked by the ideals of the parks themselves. It's just interwoven with your life."

And there's an underlying layer of some unique emotion—a mixture of pity, bewilderment and consternation—that Disney fans feel for those who don't get it, who don't understand why someone could allow a "kids' company" to occupy so much rent-free space in their heads. But it seems likely that nearly every person who has ever poo-pooed someone else's Disney vibe only does so because they haven't yet experienced it, and many of them are as reluctant to give it a try as your parents are to set up the Wi-Fi. A select few have tried the parks or other Disney products and came away unimpressed, and those few can drown out the throngs of Disney fans out there.

The criticisms are common, and some are definitely true. The lines are long. The prices are exorbitant. The heat can be oppressive. The planning can be maddening. The crowds can be overwhelming and discouraging. The combination could create a cacophony of chaos that makes you want to turn the Universe of Energy car right around and go home after your daughter loses her mind when Minnie has to take a break from signing autographs, your son wets through his clothes and leaves a fun present for the next Living with the Land rider, and everyone in the family is on your case because you've tried and failed to obtain a coveted Akershus reservation not once, not twice, but thrice … for example.

Hey, life can happen. One's presence in the Most Magical Place on Earth does not guarantee 100 percent joviality.

But once you experience that first moment of magic, none of those other things make an iota of difference. If you allow yourself to, and maybe even if you do so against your will, you get swept up in the moments that the parks create, the memories that your kids created for you and they'll carry on to their future families.

Maybe it's that sign you see when you enter the Magic Kingdom, that sign that can make a middle-aged author tear up when he thinks about it—"Here you leave today and enter the world of yesterday, tomorrow and fantasy." Or maybe it's that epochal tower summoning tourists down Main Street to the Magic Kingdom's hub, reaching higher than the wildest dreams of any child (or child at heart) who's ever spent their life waiting to get their photo taken with Mickey Mouse (THE Mickey Mouse, not some youth sports banquet or second-rate birthday knock-off). It could be that first time you ride Space Mountain, immersing yourself in an attraction experience that convinces you that you need to get married on it. Or perhaps it's seeing Spectromagic for the first time, its awe-inspiring soundtrack and choreography making you feel for the first time in your life that the old line of "If you can dream it, you can do it" is more than a cliché your parents fed to you to hide you from the grim truth of the world's many shattered wishes. And perhaps it's watching Cinderella Castle shimmer with your daughter as The Kiss Good Night portends the park close, sharing a peaceful moment after a hectic day and hoping that your daughter can be as happy in her life as she makes you in yours.

That magic never really disappears, clinging to you in some way. Maybe you still have a photo hanging on your fridge—one you made a Christmas card out of—of you and your kids with every character at the Epcot Character Spot, who surprised your family at the close of business one night with a group pic. You might have gone on a year-long weight-loss regimen in order to fit into a Buzz Lightyear T-shirt you bought for a return trip, then saw your son's head burst when he met his hero and got a photo with Buzz (and you) in matching Buzz shirts. Or maybe the photo is with your wife, taken when your son was just a glimmer in your eye and you took your bride to Walt Disney World on your honeymoon, and it's parked square in the middle of the mini-Disney shrine you keep in your basement next to a scale-model Spaceship Earth and stuffed Figment.

Once the magic is soldered to your soul, you look for any way you can to recapture it. That could be through listening to the background of your favorite park areas on a near-continual loop as you slog through another day of monotony. It might be by buying old video game consoles just so you can play the Disney-themed games that were manufactured for them. It could be by introducing your son to a favorite podcast or vlog, then discussing what he heard or saw when he started consuming those shows on his own. Or perhaps you dig through the Disney+ archives to find 55-year-old Disneyland specials just to hear Walt Disney's delightful narration when describing the latest work of his Imagineers.

For some people, rather than revolutions around the sun, years are measured by sojourns to Orange County or ... Orange County. For these people, the parks are like an inexhaustible citrus fruit, always ready to deliver one more squeeze of goodness. The thirst for more juice is not necessarily all-consuming, but it lingers in the back of the mind, like a motivational tool that occasionally comes to the forefront when you question why you're doing whatever minutiae creep up on a given day—a promise of a better tomorrow.

This text is dedicated to just such a person. A lot of people visit Disney parks, but for some of them Disney becomes a lifestyle, just as Harley-Davidson motorcycles create love at first ride for some customers and Apple users are gleefully willing to wait 36 hours in line for the new iPhone after they take their first bite. Disney parks and products bring an unparalleled level of joy to the company's fans (and open the corporation up to equally unmatched levels of micro-criticism from trolls and malcontents). Disney fans understand they can't actually spend every minute of every day at one of the parks, but there's nary another place that inspires older residents to "retire" to central Florida so they can work at Walt Disney World part time or relocate to southern California in hopes of turning a website into the next great digital sensation.

Everyone who's ever shared any Disney experience or content on the internet has a story. Yaglenski has been a regular visitor to Walt Disney World since 1974. WEDWay Radio podcasters Nate and Matt Parrish made the trip from Kansas City to Orlando multiple times a year through the 1980s and 1990s, then turned that perspective into a show in February 2009. Fellow Missourian Dan Heaton made similar treks from the opposite side of the state, visiting from St. Louis through the 1980s and 1990s before launching history-based site The Tomorrow Society in summer 2015. Lou Mongello was among the first visitors to Walt Disney World in 1971, and his frequent visits from the tri-state area turned into a book that launched as much of a conglomerate as exists in this sphere of the internet.

Regardless of how that magic manifests, though, nearly everyone who's ever visited one of the parks carries some of it home with them. And a key part of the magic is that you're generally sharing it with the most important people in your life. Whether it's your young son who's coming face-to-face with his not-so-secret crush Snow White for the first time, the technical and editorial marvel that's created by an uber-detailed 15-minute attraction or a fireworks show that made your soul also explode, Disney moments have softened the hardest of hearts and brought tears to the eyes of the stoic of souls.

"To a lot of people, the parks are more important—beyond their families—than anything else in their worlds," is how Heaton put it.

What better way to get more memorable moments than to find more people to share them with? As the past quarter-century has shown, perfect strangers can often unite through Disney and make their burgeoning virtual friendships real. This Pinocchio-like transformation has kept many people logging on for years. Internet connections are how Ohio resident Keith Brown, New Jersey resident Sean Duffy and North Carolina resident Alan Mize somehow came together in 2013 to launch Enchanted Tiki Talk, a podcast with accompanying social media feeds. North Carolinian Matt Holley joined the team shortly after Mize died of a heart attack in December 2016. [1]

"I talk to these guys more than anyone else in my wife except my wife and kids," Duffy said. "I have close friends nearby that I don't talk to as much. Until Alan passed away, we never went a day without talking to each other, at least through text. How could you meet someone on the internet and become great friends? Well, we did."

Disney is how, and count Brown among the Mouse House converts. He didn't visit Walt Disney World for the first time until 2011, when his cousins wore him down and convinced him to go despite an aversion to heat and mass gatherings. Any gruff exterior melted away as soon as he passed through the gates, though: "As soon as I saw the castle, I turned into a 10-year-old, and it's been an obsession ever since."

Parrish's wife is a fellow convert, but she is among the small subset who needed multiple trips to get there. He said she was turned off by the throngs of New Year's Eve attendees in 2004, but a follow-up trip the subsequent October yielded a better magic-to-humanity balance and she was hooked. They've taken their family pretty much every year since.

Life is full of small moments that create long-lasting impressions upon your mind. These moments are to be cherished and sought on a daily basis. But a lot of people tend to do better dealing with the day-to-day when they have something to look forward to. That's part of what made getting through the Covid-19 pandemic so tough—everything shut down pretty much at once, and there was no target date for when some sort of normalcy might come back. But once it did, people were drawn to it like water when a collapsed sponge is released into a bathtub. And trying to find a target to strive for—whether it be the reopening of the local mall, ability to eat at the corner café once again or reschedule one of the tens of thousands of canceled Disney vacations in spring 2020—was the only life raft for some people to cling to.

Even during far less trying times, the Disney parks represent such a safety net. When the parks weren't available for months—the longest stretch they've ever been closed off from the public—Disney bloggers, podcasters and vloggers stepped in to fill the void. The content may have been a bit different, but for most of them the goal—to make someone else's day a little brighter by sharing a small piece of their passion—was the same.

This text, like the countless works of so many creators on the internet, is a bit of a niche passion project, but one that deserves to be put together. It will attempt to capture a small piece of the magic that's created friendships that the internet Disneysphere has spawned. With so many options available in the 21st century, an absolutely comprehensive compendium of the Disneyverse would exhaust the world's supply of words and still be insufficient. And the rabbit hole of research involved in digging into the issue pretty much goes to infinity and beyond. But by capturing some of the players both large and small, it will hopefully serve to explain why some of the sites you listen to and read (and perhaps some you haven't yet visited) do what they do.

The good news? There is something literally for everyone. If your favorite Disney web personality is featured in these pages, hopefully it might validate your fandom. But your favorite's absence should by no means serve as a measure of insignificance. Rather, you can hopefully learn about some new storytellers and gain new nuggets of wisdom about familiar ones.

Unable to come up with that one little spark of imagination that would be a content source of substance, I decided to create this book as a way to help others capture the magic at home, like how a wanna-be athlete who discovers he can't actually dribble, hit or throw a ball decided to instead become a sportswriter. The hope was to find out what makes these people tick, how they got started and perhaps—just perhaps—spur a reader or two on to following their dream and starting a site of his or her own, to follow their Disney passion. If talking to so many authors and podcasters has taught this humble scribe anything, it's that these are passion projects in the purest sense of that phrase. Whether they have 10 listeners or 10 million, these personalities keep plugging away in hopes of improving the afternoon of at least one person—much like Walt strived to do for decades of innovation.

For them, much like for him, it all started with a mouse.

Source:

1. https://www.newsobserver.com/news/local/counties/wake-county/article123866489.html

CHAPTER TWO

The Way to Get Started: Begin Doing

Since Walter Elias Disney crossed the country a century ago to set up his eponymous animation studio with brother Roy, that family surname has been synonymous with innovation. So to consider that the Walt Disney Company was so far behind in providing a direct link between its operations and its customers once such a delivery method was so readily accessible might come as a surprise.

But the Disney Parks Blog was more than a decade late to the party when it began giving hyperactive Disneyphiles hyperlinks to company news in September 2009 (the company did have a web presence of some sort going back to the mid-1990s, with Disney.com launching in February 1996). [1] Almost as soon as Tim Berners-Lee (or Al Gore, depending on what you believe) created the World Wide Web, Disney fans began flocking to the internet. Within the first few years of the internet's widespread adoption, Disney fans were using early forums to share updates, relate to each other's reminiscences and—whether you believe this sort of activity could happen on the web or not—complain about the company's decisions. Many also used to boast about the number of parks visits they'd made by adding the number into the signatures of their AOL (yep, AOL) email accounts.

The company that brought to the world the promise of tomorrow took several years to catch up, allowing niche writers and podcasters to espouse the original concept and intent of Epcot Center (and then wax nostalgic about once-great triumphs like Horizons and CommuniCore), lament the loss of the Tomorrowland Skyway, and theorize what big hit or miss company executives would come up with next. Given that the Walt Disney Company had ABC and any number of local TV stations under its umbrella—along with a then-burgeoning cable channel of original content—it was only natural for the company to focus at that time on more traditional media. And early content creators reveled in the not-quite-outlaw nature of what they were doing during that era.

All of that chatter eventually caught the ears of Mouse House brass, though, who figured there was no better source than them. But rather than silence the cacophony of voices, that only gave so many more Disney bloggers and podcasters additional ammunition. For, rather than having to hunt for information or original ideas, they could opt (if they wished) to simply riff off of what Disney itself put out there.

Before that, though, Disney fans racked their brains for ideas in some cases, and in other cases finally had a forum for what had been a long-time passion. To precisely pin down the earliest days of Disney blogging is probably an impossible task, but the hobby does definitely predate the ability to post audio and video online—as well as to surf the web on a color computer.

Early entrants to the Disneysphere were basic, to be kind—which is understandable once you see how many of them were launched through AOL—but the passion of their entries was no less fervent. Among them:

- Disneyland Year by Year, a simple list of attractions over the years at the original Disney park (http://home.earthlink.net/~lynndenn/dl/)
- Yesterland, a tribute to discontinued Disneyland attractions (http://www.yesterland.com)
- Happiest Potties on Earth, a down-to-the-bowels deep dive on Disneyland's bathrooms (http://members.aol.com/DLPotties)
- DeWayne's Beanie Newsflash (http://www.geocities.com/~checkietrekkie/disnews.html) and Disney Beanie Report (http://www.dustie.com), two sites that fueled the fire that was the late-1990s hottest collectible-turned-failed-nest egg, the Beanie Baby
- Magical Music of the Mouse, a tres-1990s complete Disney CD list (http://magicmusic.net)
- Jungle Gnus Report, a message board and interview site for former Jungle Cruise skippers that was slightly less captivating than an alligator playing with an elephant (http://www.junglecruise.com—Disney, which created the Jungle Cruise and would likely love to have the use of its namesake url to promote its forthcoming movie, does not own the junglecruise.com URL)
- Disney's California Adventure Virtual Tour, can't say for sure if it included Superstar Limo (http://members.xoom.com/rocketrod16)
- Chef Mayhem's Unofficial Tribute to the Haunted Mansion, one of many tributes to Disney's 999 happy haunts (http://www.doombuggies.com)
- MMC Online, a fan site devoted to the Justin Timberlake/Christina Aguilera/Britney Spears-era Mickey Mouse Club (http://www.multiboard.com/~spettit/mmc)

- Disney Characters and Stuff, a collection of photos of Disneyland's costumed characters (http://www.toonfinder.com)
- Unofficial Disney Animation Archive, which is pretty self-explanatory (http://come.to/disneyarchive)
- Brian Bennett's Disney Trip Planner, an early resource guide for travelers featuring tips and tricks (http://members.aol.com/dvclubber/dvchome.htm)
- Kiara's Sahifa, dedicated to Simba and Nala's daughter (the cub held up by Rafiki at the end of "The Lion King") (http://www.lionking.org/~kiara/main.html)
- Deb's Unofficial Walt Disney World Information Guide, an online resource set up by Deb Wills to help readers' vacations be as magical as possible (http://wdwig.com)

Wills would end up being perhaps the most prolific early opiner on all things Disney. She began writing online in 1996 and formed what would become All Ears, an amalgamation of a website whose blog posts and reviews drew eight-figure monthly page visits as well as an email newsletter with a six-figure subscribership. [2, 3] Like so many people who devote themselves to taking up bandwidth with their Disney content, Wills was inspired in her youth by all things Disney, making sure to tune in to "Wonderful World of Disney" every week and even getting to attend the 1964 World's Fair in New York City—which any Disney fan worth his or her ears knows as Walt Disney's personal playground and testing ground to theme park mainstays such as It's a Small World and Great Moments with Mr. Lincoln. [4]

Wills occasionally wrote about other travels she took, but the bulk of her bylines pertains to

Disney-related content. She was one of the first to focus on Disney Cruise Lines, painstakingly describing her preparations weeks ahead of time and eventually becoming one of the main sources of travel tips both for the cruises and Disney Parks. While previous generations couldn't escape fast enough when their aunts and uncles busted out the slide projector to show photos of their trip to Mount Vernon, Disney fans in the internet age have for decades had a hunger for Mouse House content that couldn't be filled by all the trays of food at Tusker House. And Wills catered exactly to that craving, offering information on everything from baby birds growing up at the former Disney-MGM Studios to a port-by-port evaluation of every stop on a Mediterranean cruise.

Not everyone can afford an overseas trip, of course, but many people dream of flying south or west to visit a domestic park. Mary Waring, wanting to pass on savings for those trips for her friends and family, founded a private site that shared Disney discounts. The page grew so much that, within three months of its February 2001 founding, she had to revamp it and take it public. Thus, Mouse Savers was form. Demand surged for people seeking trip information, so she quickly added pages for different parks, other Disney destinations and Disney merchandise. It had secured the ability to negotiate special rates at Walt Disney World hotels within a year of its founding. [5]

While people spend a lot of time planning for and reveling in their trips, many take pure pleasure in hearing about others' experiences with the parks and the company. Wills, aside from chronicling her travel escapades, ultimately wanted to bridge connections between fans of all types. She said she got started in order to keep updated on and hear from fellow fans of the parks. As she told the Hartford Courant, "People wanted more and more information ... The very first Disney site I found online was two pages—thought I had died and gone to heaven." [6] She added some of the internet's first parks FAQ pages and menu discussion forums, as well, learning about the latest goings-on from first-hand confirmation as well as submitted trip reports.

Among those to connect with her and her site was John Frost, who at the time was living in southern California but had been posting in UseNet groups since he first became aware of the internet in about 1992. In a phone interview, Frost said he began seeking out other Disney fans while attending Lewis and Clark College in Portland, Oregon, in the mid-1990s. He also wrote FAQ pieces about various park attractions. By the late-1990s, he and other fans who'd connected online were regularly meeting at the parks looking to broaden their reach. He helped organize many such events, including a weekly Sunday afternoon meet-up at Disneyland. He also met his wife at a Disney event and married her on Disney property.

"We looked across the U.S., and we saw there were three or four other sites writing about Disney World," said Frost, who caught on with Doobie Moseley and began writing for Laughing Place, the site Moseley founded in 1999 with his wife Rebekah. [7]

Frost grew up in a Disney family. His grandfather, Vic Greene, was recruited by Walt Disney himself to work for the company starting in 1954. Greene painted flats in the old Indian Village at Disneyland, but his engineering background came through with his work on mainstay attractions like the Matterhorn. He was left in charge by Walt Disney of Disneyland during the World's Fair, according to Frost, and was eventually moved over to Project X, which became Walt Disney World. [8] He is among those Imagineers whose names have been immortalized on Main Street USA; his name is chillin' above the ice cream shop. Frost's mother and aunt, meanwhile, also worked at Disneyland in their youths, so he regularly made the trek down the Pacific coast from Oregon to Anaheim throughout his childhood.

Without much of a blueprint for how to do the internet—and with mainstream media essentially ignoring digital news delivery entirely for years—early Disney content creators were free to make their respective sites in pretty much any form they saw fit. In Frost's case, his unique background combined with his quickly growing writing credentials helped him, Laughing Place and the Disney blogging community as a whole gain some needed credibility in the late-1990s. Much of the Disney online content up until this point was focused on tributes to the parks or trip visits, but Frost felt there was a niche to be carved in offering continuous theme park and company news. So he mostly played it straight, offering regular updates and devoting himself to being a main source of theme park information.

"I had connections at Disneyland. Cynthia Harriss was the president of Disneyland then, and I was on the advisory council. They were doing a window dedication on Main Street. She saw me and came over and said, 'What are you doing on that side of the rope? You should be over here,' and she escorted us to the press area," Frost said.

That led to the online Disney community being welcomed as part of the press, with the first Disneyland event to which bloggers were officially invited being the celebration of the 1999 U.S. Women's World Cup-winning soccer team at Disneyland. But without the luxuries that modern hardware and software offered, blogging back then didn't quite deliver the speed to which consumers would become accustomed.

"We got scooped on that by the L.A. Times because their time to press was shorter," Frost said in what's probably the most unexpected thing you'll read this week. "We had no (content management system) software back then, so we had to edit everything by hand."

Over on the East Coast, Yaglenski was similarly earning access through Disney's golden gates. A former radio voice talent, he got a job in the mid-1990s as an assistant at a real estate company. He's gotten a taste of computers, but during his tenure there he was the first person in the office to buy his own computer (a two-MB Hewlett-Packard) and to get his own email address. His curiosity grew as the internet slowly became more a part of people's lives—as did his tech needs, as that Hewlett-Packard outlived its usefulness in six months—so he dabbled in web development, writing the code to develop a directory of local businesses. The regional internet provider he did business with in Maryland, Levelbest Communications, ended up hiring him as its general manager of web development—a job that brought with it a lot of free time in an era when few sites existed and those that did were little more than digital business cards.

"The phone didn't ring a whole lot. That us to trying to hone our skills on developing something," he said in a video interview. "So I thought, 'What do I know a lot about?' Disney was one of those things."

All he needed was a name. Wanting to promote a communal feel and ties to Walt Disney's vision, he settled upon the Internet Community of Tomorrow. InterCOT started in October 1997 as a listing of attractions, but it grew to include park ride and videos from the trips Yaglenski took with his family to Walt Disney World starting in 1974 (those were $25-per-night trips to the Polynesian Resort during which his dad declined to buy a $1,000 lifetime pass). That made

InterCOT one of the internet's earliest users of video, which was no easy task while the population has access to nothing more powerful than a 56K modem: "It would buffer 20 times while you watched it." Those simplistic POV videos and some skillful metatagging quickly got InterCOT among the top three Yahoo search results for Disney—ahead of the Walt Disney Company's own travel site. To further illustrate the site's age, it was also a hit on AltaVista—which Yahoo acquired in 2003—Excite (which was the fourth-most popular site on the internet in 2000 but will likely have to be Googled by anyone who's accustomed to using the word "Google" as a verb) and the oldest surviving internet search engine, WebCrawler. Once Google became a ubiquitous part of life in the early-2000s, InterCOT also worked its way up to No. 2 in its rankings, netting 9.3 million hits and more than 300,000 unique visitors per month. [9]

"That led to a lot of emails from travelers asking questions about their trip packages and such," he said. "I put this site up, and magically traffic started appearing. Back then, you could do that. You'd put up a site about something, and people would find it because there was so little on the internet."

One of the main UseNet groups—one to which these and many other creators belonged in the 1990s—was rec.arts.disney.parks. The group spawned what was likely the first internet meetup in December 1996, bringing together about 20 people mainly from the central Florida area. The event grew within a few years to incorporate more than 300 fans per event from across the globe; meetups continued at least into 2019, with Covid-19 challenging those and pretty much everything else in 2020 and beyond.[10] The discussion group itself also has survived into the 2020s, via Google (you can check it out at groups.google.

com/group/rec.arts.disneyparks). Active discussions on more than 130,000 topics prove that, for all of the modern conveniences and outlets available to them, Disney fans can't help but stay engaged through these old-school means.

The ongoing interest of forums like that showed there was plenty of room on the internet for more, easier-to-use means of sharing thoughts with each other. Yaglenski grew his site's community aspect out by putting together a rudimentary discussion board. It garnered a good deal of attention within days, and before long distinct pages had to be set up for each topic—a nearly unheard-of concept in the late-1990s. He soon had to bring on a couple moderators and was pleasantly overwhelmed by the traction the site generated.

That includes financial. InterCOT never has been Yaglenski's full-time job, but it was one of the first Disney sites to gain advertisers, albeit low-revenue ones (among its first advertisers—CD Now, which billed itself as "The internet's number one music store," and a fledgling online bookstore called amazon.com). [11] After finding some better discussion software and a server that was one of the first to be able to accommodate video, the site became one of the web's early go-to Disney resources. But the relatively high-tech tools and the revenue stream were all means to an end for Yaglenski, who wanted to unite the Disney online universe. He called discussion forums like his "the original Facebook" for the ways in which they brought people together.

"Within the first five years of being online, we were doing 2 million visitors a month. But we had almost no way to monetize it. In the early days, there wasn't Google AdSense," he said.

There was, however, a wealth of opportunity. Yaglenski was one of the first internet content creators to be invited to a Walt Disney World press event, the opening of the Cinderella Castle suite in 2006. Having relocated to Hilton Head, S.C., he's still close enough to drive to central Florida to cover events and avails himself of the opportunity whenever possible.

"That was my first indication that, 'Hey, this could be something really cool beyond just having a website,'" said Yaglenski, who noted that Disney flew him down to Florida as part of the event. "Disney was actually recognizing us."

Indeed, early sites like these showed print journalists that the rarefied air of all-access privileges they enjoyed wasn't going to be nearly as exclusive as it once was. Jim Hill saw the conversion begin while he worked as a print journalist in the 1990s, then he jumped to the Dark Side by the turn of the 21st century. Hill has, for the most part, covered Disney operations from his home base of New Boston, N.H., since 1984, after a stint as an Army journalist during which his fellow soldiers knew him as "the Disney geek." That's when he bylined his first Disney piece, a feature on Donald Duck's "retirement ceremony" from the Army to coincide with the character's 50th anniversary (Donald was featured as a soldier in numerous propaganda war-themed cartoons during the World War II era, but a check of Disney's archives showed that he never officially left the service). [12] In a phone interview, Hill said he rewrote a friend's article for the subject with her permission, and that story on Sergeant Donald's ceremony (he was promoted from private upon discharge) before a 1,500-troop review garnered international attention when it was picked up by The Associated Press. From there, he was invited by the Walt Disney Company to cover Disneyland's 30th anniversary the following year.

"That trip was sort of my first introduction to that professional arc," Hill said of that 1985 jaunt. "Two men in front of me started to talk about being there opening day. I said, 'You're (former Disney artist) John Hench, and you're (former Imagineer) Harper Goth. They then became my first Imagineer 'gets.' " [13, 14]

He then clawed out a career for more than a decade covering Disney for various publications, making connections with the likes of former animator Mark Davis, as well as longtime Imagineers Bruce Gordon and Tony Baxter—names that weren't quite as familiar to Disney fans who had to reply upon print products during what Hill called "the Paleozoic Era of Disney fandom." But in 1998 Hill got a taste of the next generation when he was recruited by Al Lutz to write a review of Michael Eisner's 1998 autobiography "Work in Progress" for a site Lutz ran that was known as Disneyland Information Guide. And he didn't have the turnaround issues that cost Frost his scoop.

"I was used to articles appearing weeks later. I handed off the book review and then like an hour later, I got a note saying it was up. It was up and edited. It's everything I wrote, and it's up on the web in an hour, and there's immediate feedback. That was the first little taste of heroin."

Disney Information Guide was spawned after years of Lutz posting in various Usenet groups, with what began as a schedule site (it claimed to be more updated than Disney's own Disneyland online guide) going on to contain a wealth of travel resources and Disneyland news. [15] It went on to become Mouse Planet (which Lutz left to start Mice Chat), and Hill went on to write thrice-weekly columns for that site for several years. He had to get accustomed to having Disney brass reach out to offer praise and criticism—he said senior management at Disney kept up on web mentions back then because there were so few blogs at the time and the company didn't have a web presence of its own, to speak of.

The work of pioneers like Hill and Frost helped build up their credibility, which in turn made bloggers a central part of the Disneysphere. The opening of Disney's Animal Kingdom at Walt Disney World in 1998 and Disney's California Adventure, the second gate at Disneyland, in 2001 gave bloggers a chance to flex their muscles in terms of what they could offer to their readers. Sites like Mouse Planet focused on covering every conceivable angle of the DCA development, to the point that a creative difference between Hill and Lutz over a need to diversify led to their parting ways. But they and other sites like Laughing Place also sprinkled in criticism, proving they could be impartial and not beholden to Disney even as they fought to gain the respect of the company and its followers.

Lutz, in fact, became known as a main source of criticism in large part because of what he perceived to be the fantastic flop of early DCA. His frequent accuracy worried company executives and gained him a solid following of readers and journalists alike. His "Promote Paul Pressler" page pushed the notion of the then-head of Disneyland to be promoted out of that job entirely. And if there was anything else he disliked at the Anaheim property—the McDonald's fry push card, a dearth of merchandise, a wayward-looking piece of furniture—he was there to cover it, smiling and winking the whole time (not the emoji of a person winking, but the semicolon sort of wink, as emojis weren't a thing yet). [16, 17] His voice compelled the Walt Disney Company, at least according to a Medium report, to usurp the Al Lutz name for its own gain, pushing certain company-approved narratives that may have helped bolster the push to remove Michael Eisner from power (the company never commented on the report, and several parties involved questioned parts of the report). [18]

Nonetheless, Lutz's success and the success of other pioneers like him paved the way for online content creators. They gained the respect of mainstream media, who before long were using bloggers as official sources on harder stories such as Market Watch's reports on DCA's early struggles. [19] Frost's coverage of hurricanes Charley, Frances and Jeanne in the 2004 hurricane season—just months after he launched the Disney Blog—proved that internet content creators could lead the way on major stories and resulted in a fivefold increase in his nascent site's traffic once it got rolling.

Internet sites also brought stories relating the parks much more to life for the creators and audiences alike. While stories about new attractions and renovations might generate a few inches of coverage from the newspapers, the limited focus and unlimited space on the internet allowed members of the Disneysphere to devote multiple stories per day for weeks at a time, allowing for every nuance and historical perspective to be rolled into part of the coverage package. And as forums and comment sections got more sophisticated, the audience could be a part of the process, whether to share praise of a move, memories of a closing attraction or troll before trolling was known as such.

All of this combined to give early content creators an air of credibility and respect with audiences and mainstream media alike. It's also a part of why many outlets, including the daily newspapers in the Los Angeles and Orlando areas and Orlando Business Journal, now have writers whose beats partially or completely entail covering those areas' theme parks. Before that earned credibility, though, those who were part of the Disneysphere reveled in what they were creating. They ultimately proved that Disney fandom is a small world, after all.

"It was just a really exciting time back then, the first 10 years from 1999-2009 where there was a pretty small group of people," Frost said. "We all helped each other out, got to see each other. A bunch lived in (Washington) D.C., some in Chicago, some in New York."

Sites like InterCOT gave the followers of the Disney content creators a chance to be heard, as well. Before the days of social media, discussion boards were just about the only way for fans to share their thoughts on all things Disney. Yaglenski said he's proud that he's been able to hold true to Walt Disney's personal philosophy about business, maintaining a family-friendly forum and issuing warnings (and then banishments) to those who violated the policy.

There is a huge difference, however, between maintaining a positive tone and toeing the company line. Every content creator who was interviewed for this work agreed that maintaining a sense of autonomy from Disney plays a huge role in whatever longevity they may enjoy (lest they risk becoming embroiled in a Lutz-style controversy of their own). Aside from a lack of consistency, most agreed that early sites that have since gone the way of Bambi's mother, Jasmine's mother and ... well, the mother of nearly every other Disney main character couldn't adequately maintain the sort of independence that builds credibility. An audience, in and of itself, doesn't guarantee a site's success or failure. But for someone who might already be on the fence, like some of the sites listed earlier, seeing declined interest that could result from being too rah-rah could be enough to convince them to move on to the next project.

Other times, it might have been a shifting of life priorities or a general loss of interest that added another site to the digital graveyard. But every early content creator helped give one little spark of imagination to at least one other consumer, some of whom went on to be part of the next, much larger wave of the Disneysphere. The death of a blog or podcast didn't—and doesn't—necessarily mean that the creator's passion for Disney has dissipated. It simply means they're searching for another way to share that fervor with the world. Even those who have persevered have their moments of uncertainty.

"I feel very grateful to have had that opportunity," Frost said. "Even when I start questioning how much more do I want to do this, I go to events like Star Wars and Mickey and Minnie. The Disney fan in you wakes up, and you're energized again."

Those who have been able to power on into a new generation carry a lot of respect for some of their early peers and competitors. They're also thankful to the fans who've stuck with them into middle age and beyond, in many cases sharing their passion for the parks with children who can't imagine the type of world where a person had to struggle to find a fellow Disney fan.

"People have gotten married after meeting through my site. This is what I built. This is my legacy—and it's not an ugly monolith in front of Epcot," Yaglenski said.

Sources:

1. https://disneyparks.disney.go.com/blog/
2. https://www.chicagotribune.com/travel/os-et-disney-all-ears-deb-wills-20180719-story.html
3. https://allears.net/walt-disney-world/wdw-planning/meet-deb-wills/
4. https://disneyparks.disney.go.com/blog/2011/04/the-1964-new-york-worlds-fair-a-new-disney-technology-is-born/

5. https://www.mousesavers.com/about-mousesavers-com/
6. https://www.courant.com/os-cfb-talking-with-deb-willis-20160228-story.html
7. https://www.laughingplace.com/w/author/doobie_moseley
8. https://www.businessinsider.com/walt-disneys-original-plan-for-epcot-2015-5
9. https://www.frederi.com/archives/urbana-web-firm-experts-on-disney/article_d17e9708-465a-5c7b-81ab-134ec78f5774.html
10. http://meets.radp.org/
11. https://web.archive.org/web/19981111184439/http://www.intercot.com/
12. https://www.telegraph.co.uk/culture/tvandradio/11834429/How-Donald-Duck-helped-win-Second-World-War-and-beat-Mickey-to-the-job.html
13. https://d23.com/walt-disney-legend/john-hench/
14. https://d23.com/walt-disney-legend/harper-goff/
15. https://web.archive.org/web/19981202081323/http://members.aol.com/alweho/docs/contents.htm
16. https://medium.com/@snydergary310/the-dis-influencer-2ec902b53c77
17. http://www.emuck.com:3000/archive/lutz
18. https://madnesskingdom.com/gary-snyders-wild-ride-51e6d74d4cea
19. http://web.archive.org/web/20140222204145/https://www.marketwatch.com/story/no-gold-rush-for-california-adventure

CHAPTER THREE

Think, Dream, Believe, Dare

There's no real way to quantify a "biggest" or a "greatest" in the Disney blogosphere. But among almost everyone who was generous enough to share their time and their story for this book, one name repeatedly came up—often when asked who influenced the various content creators who were interviewed, sometimes completely unprovoked. Some appreciate his longevity, others his positivity. Still others credit him for inspiring them to get into the Disneysphere at all.

"Lou was smart and created something amazing. He's like a unicorn," Heaton said.

Lou, of course, refers to Lou Mongello, creator of WDW Radio. The Plainfield, New Jersey, native parlayed a lifelong love of Disney and a calculated 1,000-mile leap of faith to create what might be the pre-eminent Disney content source—making WDW Radio to Disney podcasting what Kleenex is to facial tissues and Xerox is (was?) to copy machines. During a phone interview that was secured after weeks of wrangling—a credit to the many hats he has to wear as part of his enterprise—Mongello was loath to take the credit that such a reputation might warrant.

"I built the clubhouse, but it's the people that populate it," he said. "When I got started, I had zero expectations."

That start was sparked by those previously mentioned childhood visits. The Mongello family ventured south to Florida on what he described as Griswold-style jaunts every year once Walt Disney World was open. Prior to that, he was hooked by watching "The Wonderful World of Disney" with his family every Sunday night. He maintained that passion for Disney through adolescence and into adulthood, even as life took him in other directions—including his other passion, law. Mongello became a practicing attorney in New Jersey after earning a law degree from Seton Hall University. Never one to be content with only one hustle, Mongello also opened a computer consulting and web design company called Imagine Enterprises, as well as working for a time as the chief technology officer for a medical imaging company called Tricat Radiology.

But what many people would call a full plate he still considered half-empty.

"I loved the idea of being able to help people, but I didn't realize at the time (law) wasn't fueling my fire," he told Desperate Housegeek. "It wasn't fueling my passion. I wasn't excited to get up and run to work to argue with people and fight with other lawyers." [1]

But there was that OTHER passion still percolating in the back of his mind. In adulthood, Mongello was a member of the New Jersey, national and world chapters of the National Fantasy Fan Club, whose goal was to share the Disney legacy. Just because, he also completed the College of Disney Knowledge and completed certification to serve as a Disney Specialist. [2] Mongello got the urge in the early-2000s to write a book. The topic of that book was obvious ... eventually.

"I wasn't smart enough to write about computers or technology. The only thing I knew about was Disney. And having spent so much time there and reading about the parks, I got to know a lot of the hidden details," he said. "Even when I asked my wife about me writing a book, her response to me was, 'The only thing you know about is Disney World.' "

Seeing that there weren't a lot of books relating to parks trivia on the market at that time, he decided to jump full bore into a Disney project. He got every travel book he could find at Barnes and Noble, obtained those publishers' information and sent out a pitch for his book. About 40 pitches were sent; one acceptance letter, from The Intrepid Traveler, came back. Thus, "The Walt Disney World Trivia Book" turned from wish to reality in 2004 and was the first step in making Mongello the most successful .025 hitter in history. The book broke questions and factoids out by park and land, prompting the reader to figure out queries such as how many artificial leaves are on the Tree of Life and what's at the very top of Spaceship Earth.

Mongello had already taken his passion to the internet by that point. A few months after the book hit shelves (you know, back when books existed only in paper form), Mongello launched a Disney World Trivia website in large part to promote the book. That site also featured discussion forums on most any Disney-related topic and took off in a way that Mongello couldn't have anticipated.

"We had 29 people on that first site. That 29 turned into 500, 1,000, 10,000, 50,000. That got me thinking, 'Wait a minute. There's a lot of people out there like me,' " he said.

There were a lot of people who wanted to read about Disney and, it turned out, a lot of people whose ears were burning for some Disney content. Mongello partnered with Nathan Rose of magicalmountain.net on the Mouse Tunes Podcast, where they entertained their "podpeople" listeners with more than 60 episodes featuring Disney news, interviews and convention coverage, creating a script of sorts upon which thousands of other shows have since spun off. [3]

"When I first started out, I was one of two or maybe three podcasters in the space," Mongello said. "I had to literally go Ask Jeeves what a podcast was. That was in 2005. I knew that the spoken word was way more powerful than anything I could write."

The two parted ways in February 2007, not long after willing the 2006 Best Travel Podcast People's Choice Award (winning awards would become a theme for Mongello). He was anxious to begin a new project he called WDW Radio. That project, he felt, called for him to be much closer to the source.

"In 2007, I'm loving what I'm doing and I'm seeing it be well-received. I don't know how. I don't have a business plan. But I do know I have to give it a shot. I had fear, not of failure but that after 5, 10, 20 years had gone by, I'd wonder what would have happened if I'd given that Disney thing a shot," he said. "I'd found myself flying back and forth every few months, then ever month, then a couple times a month. Because what I was doing was associated with Disney, there was a certain standard and level in terms of what I was putting out. I needed to come down here, boots on the ground, to do research, to be in the place, and to have access to come here more often was awesome in terms of content creation."

Taking a leap so large that it involved moving into a house sight unseen, Mongello took his family to central Florida to support his new project. Mongello credits his technology background and his extensive (at least for the times) work with previous projects for giving WDW Radio an early boost. The podcast and blog associated with the operation were immediate hits. He was also among the first content creators to produce regular live video shows, having to lug a laptop and web camera through the parks while enduring the sorts of stares generally reserved for 10-car pileups and fielding quizzical queries from cast members.

"Live video is not only the most authentic medium because you can't hide what you look or feel like, but you also get that immediate reaction and that feedback from the community," he said. "But it's good to do a lot. I tried to find other ways to create content that people are comfortable listening to. My mom wouldn't be very comfortable listening to a podcast."

That podcast and the WDW Radio blog became a full-time business for Mongello, as enough advertisers took notice to make it a profitable endeavor. He declined to directly state what sort of workforce he might have, but he heaped credit upon his wife Deanna and two kids: "My family are not employees, but having a remarkable support system like them—there's no way I'd be here without them." He also shares credit with friends he's made through the business—friends he said he was devoid of through his youth, which in part accounts for his technical prowess since he had nothing better to do – who have offered help through writing blog posts, offering support and other contributions.

But Mongello has never been one to stand still, juggling a workload that most people would need more arms than General Grievous has to manage. Just as he grew adept at one thing, Mongello would start doing something else. One book became three, with another trivia book being accompanied by a guide on saving money at Walt Disney World. Mongello's expertise got him noticed by national media outlets, who made him a frequent interview subject (Mongello has also written pieces for *People* magazine). Mongello even took part in cruises which featured him as a guest of honor.

If a cruise isn't up your alley, Mongello has hosted monthly Walt Disney World meet-ups since 2008 so he can "meet listeners, shake their hands and hear their stories. I believe that nothing beats a handshake and a hug." He kept the tradition alive virtually, hosting online meet-ups during the Covid-19 pandemic with his friends, which is how he refers to everyone who listens or reaches out to him "whether we've met yet or not." He also takes the time to personally respond to every social media comment and email (another reason it could take weeks to coordinate a book interview), believing all of his "friends" deserve that personal touch rather than having that part of the job outsourced.

If you haven't gathered by this point, Mongello generally enjoys speaking. Further advancing that idea, his podcasts were soon complemented by audio guides of Walt Disney World. Mongello said he began doing those based on the same premise as his trivia books—to enhance the consumer's understanding and enjoyment of the parks. They guide the listener on a virtual trip through the parks complete with ambient noise, creating what he aimed to be a pleasurable experience both for a user at home and one who's using it in the park. His goal is to create one for each land in each park, but given the work involved with each one—researching the material, writing a script, recording, paring it down so that it (back in the day) could fit on a CD—it takes around a year to complete one, making the achievement of that goal a near-impossibility.

Mongello would likely never think that, though, just like he wouldn't think anyone else's desires were unachievable. Soon after moving down to Florida, Mongello also launched a motivational speaking enterprise that sees him address crowds at conferences and other events. The goal of this—helping people turn what they love into what they do—is a variation on what he said has been his lifelong goal.

"As you start getting older, you start to think about legacy and what you're leaving behind. I was a plaintiff attorney. I wanted to help people with tech, so I started an IT consulting company. Now I want to help people make their Disney experiences better. I help people find motivation in life. To know I've had a positive experience and helped others do the same, it's been the greatest reward," he said.

Maintaining a positive outlook is among the key points he tries to reinforce. And he tries to live that way, even when challenges like coronavirus present themselves. That time period, as it did with pretty much everybody else, wreaked havoc on his operations. But he didn't treated it that way.

"It was also a time of great opportunity," said Mongello, who said he tried to emphasize the need to find something good in any situation—like, for example, writing a book about Disney content creators when society pretty much shuts down. "This gave a lot of people the time they said they never had. That's what I tried to do is use this opportunity to make myself better, to make my business better. You have to innovate."

The financial reward for his innovation varies, but overall Mongello estimates that roughly 50 percent of his income is derived from his speaking and entrepreneurial enterprise, and the other 50 percent comes from WDW Radio and related Disney operations. That can vary depending on the circumstances, though; Covid-19, for example, pretty much wiped out his speaking engagements through much of 2020.

It took a long time to get to the point where monetization was a serious option, of course. Mongello's first piece of advice to those who seek his help: Stay the course.

"That's one of the greatest takeaways, for me, is knowing that. You can't find a blueprint or crack a code or hack the system to get more downloads, to get more views. There is none. It's passion and patience and persistence. It has to come from a real place. What people don't see are the late nights, the sacrifices, the fears and the tears. It's not easy. I love what I do. I wouldn't trade it for the world. But it is work."

Mongello is compensated more handsomely than some of his counterparts, but this relative Scrooge McDuck isn't in it for the money, he insists. Like most successful people, his reward comes from the work itself and the connections that result from it. For some people, having the likes of Marvel Studios President Kevin Feige among your fan base, Richard Sherman (half of the Sherman Brothers composing duo, not the NFL cornerback) among your friends and actress Julie Andrews among your interview credits would perhaps be rewarding. Others might take a lot of pride in winning the Best Travel Podcast Award nine straight years at the New Media Expo. Still others would consider having a top-five podcast on iTunes to be a crowning achievement. But laurel-resting isn't really his thing: "I'm never worried about the thing I'm doing. I'm worried about what's next."

The urge to think about what's next can be strong at Walt Disney World, where well-versed fans might have their minute-by-minute 10-day itineraries shared with every family member via spreadsheet. But Mongello—who admittedly has the advantage of living near the Most Magical Place on Earth—said stopping to take in some of the park's hidden gems can create great memories by living in the moment. Mongello said some of his most enjoyable visits are ones during which he doesn't get on a single attraction. Rather, he enjoys the ambience of places like Katsura Grill in the Japan pavilion of World Showcase, admiring the nearby waterfall and bamboo forest while people-watching for a bit.

"The theme parks become your park," he said. "It's where you go to hang out with friends, where you go to relax. Walt Disney World is my home."

In a more general sense, what's next—at least for the foreseeable future—is continuing to go home while producing WDW Radio and its related pursuits. He still enjoys getting up each day, in large part because they're all different. One day might require hours' worth of research on a given show topic. Another day might call for him to broadcast live videos from an attraction or land opening. And yet another day could see him in front of conventioneers from around the country trying to get them to be their best selves.

So he has every reason in the world to keep going.

"I hope I can. If one person listens, I'll continue doing it. At some point, if it stops becoming fun, then we see what's next. The road to where I got now is very circuitous. You never know what might come in the future. I would be the luckiest man in the universe if I continue doing this. I measure it in levels of happiness. And I am happy."

Sources:

1. https://www.desperatehousegeek.com/lou-mongello-wdw-radio/
2. https://web.archive.org/web/20090831131005/http://www.wdwradio.com/About-the-Author-Lou-Mongello.html
3. https://web.archive.org/web/20070209083834/http://www.mousetunes.com/shownotes/mousetunes_020407.php

CHAPTER FOUR

Moving Forward, Opening New Doors, Doing New Things

Townie is often used as a derogatory term, but most people who live in the greater Orlando area likely take a great deal of pride in their residency.

Like Ariel's voice captured the heart and mind of Prince Eric, Walt Disney World has served as a siren's call to attract people of all sorts to central Florida to be around, and in many cases earn some kind of living due to, the Happiest Place on Earth. There's even a 10,000-member Facebook group devoted to people who want to move to Orlando to be closer to Disney. Some, like Mongello, dropped everything else in their lives to devote their attention to a lifelong passion (Mongello devoted an episode of WDW Radio to the topic, hosting a roundtable with people who similarly set off for the Sunshine State).

Others, like Serena Lyn, literally move to Florida just to write about the experience of moving to Florida. A web designer and social media marketer, she moved from Virginia to Orlando in November 2015 to write about the experience of living next to Walt Disney World (she boasts that she can see the park's fireworks from her house). [1] The site she launched to chronicle the experience, Living By Disney, chronicles the experience of the parks and moving to central

Florida while also offering travel tips and other advice (living near Walt Disney World has self-explanatory perks, she said, but traffic and weaving through tourists when you live there can be a hassle).

Wills was a neighbor of Yaglenski in Maryland until 2012, when she moved to Orlando to be closer to the action. [2] She was helped by having built about 15 years of credibility on All Ears before migrating south. Uprooting for what some people might consider to be a pipe dream isn't for everyone; as Hill put it, "Being that close to the candy shop sometimes makes people a little nuts." But in Yaglenski's opinion, location isn't just the first commandment of real estate: "In the original days, that didn't make a big difference. Now in the last five to seven years, it's a bigger thing to live there. You can be throwing up content that has today's picture from wherever ... I'm still competing with people who are literally three minutes from the park."

Tom Corless may not live quite that close, but his move down the eastern seaboard—combined with a labored effort that makes Aurora's slumber seem like a catnap—helped him become one of the go-to Disney sources in the 2010s. The Bronx native—you may sense a theme here—was born into Disney fandom, visiting the U.S. parks at least four times a year through his childhood. But he got a late start online, not having internet access until 2003.

"Once I was on there, I realized, 'Oh, hey, there's a Disney fandom thing going on on the internet,' " he said in a phone interview.

Corless was active on various forums and kept abreast of Disney happenings through his time in the journalism school at Iona College, where he was recruited to be part of a Disney-related email newsletter. He figured any chance to gain writing experience was good—no matter how brief.

"I thought it'd be fun to write something that was fun. But the thing is, people fall out of love with stuff very quickly and vanish," he said. "After about six weeks, (the newsletter founders) vanished. I liked having that outlet. We had a couple thousand readers. I was getting a lot of feedback."

So he decided to buy a website. He acquired a domain name and hosting services, but the result was "the ugliest website ever made," by his own words. Indeed, the site that billed itself as "A Whole New World of News!!!" (because all reputable websites rely upon a triumvirate of exclamation points to emphasize their credibility) featured a series of words that may or may not have been spelled correctly, in an order that sometimes resembled proper English (without much need for pesky punctuation), in fonts that changed from paragraph to paragraph.

Nonetheless, in July 2007, WDW News Today was born. And any lack of design competency was more than made up for with confidence, as Corless' first post ended with, "Thanks for reading the soon to be #1 source for Walt Disney World news!" (the site really loved exclamation points). [3]

"The host company had this content software. You entered text, and the site put it together. It was hideous. I think we had midi music, and I was quickly told that was a terrible idea," he said. "The front page was just a running blog of news, just a homepage that kept growing. You'd have a date with a couple bullet points of the day's news."

Corless did link to Mongello, Hill and other early Disney content creators, as well. And the site featured one of the earliest Disney-related podcasts, launching before the end of that first summer of operation. The WDW News Today Podcast only appeared once a month in its early days, offering a roundup of the latest

Disney news of the time, but before long it featured numerous new episodes a week. By December of that year, someone offered to convert WDW News Today to a Wordpress-accessible site, giving it the look that Corless said more closely resembles its current layout. He also recruited some extra hands, including photographers, by the time 2008 rolled around. Corless was in New York City when he launched the site, but he had a couple people turning around content for him in Orlando before the site's first anniversary.

"A lot of us were young and didn't have lives. I'd be on Skype most evenings, and whoever wasn't busy would chime in. The rest of the night would become this weird social group," he said.

He grew a small following of hardcore fans, but it remained firmly entrenched in hobby status well into the next decade despite turtle-paced upward trajectory. That growth was buoyed by the steadfastness of Corless and his troupe of volunteers, who chipped away in the mine, where the million virtual diamonds shine, and made the site the first to feature posts every single day. Corless moved to Orlando in May 2013 to help support his fun but unprofitable hobby, but he had little else. Intermittent job prospects in his preferred field of journalism fell through. And yet he just kept swimming until 2016, when his site's Marlin found its Crush and caught its Eastern Australian Current of profitability.

"Everyone always felt like we were doing a really good job. We were having triple-digit increases, all of this money coming in. And it hit me: I think this is a profitable business right now," he said.

Corless continued to expand the site's reach along with its profit margins. Before long, he dedicated sections to every Disney Parks location in the world, as well as television and movie projects from Disney properties, Broadway and radio. The WDW News Today podcast network also expanded, adding niche programs Radio Free Disneyland (focused on historical topics), Nerd Alert Podcast (featuring talk about "Star Wars" and the Marvel Cinematic Universe) and Ride Rehab (during which hosts watch vintage Disney programming and offer commentary). The site also became one of the first to list attraction refurbishments and park hours, and there was enough demand to warrant a dedicated WDW News Today app and online radio station that features original programs and Disney Parks music. He hires designers and app developers per-project for work like that, and Corless oversees a staff of eight full-time employees and 10 part-time workers. But being a boss is hardly what motivates him.

"That's the part of it I hate. I handle the content side. I didn't go to business school," he said. "Luckily, I have people who are good with that stuff."

And Corless has shown he's pretty good at his stuff, proving that he and his staff are "the most hardcore of the hardcore fans." Included in the site's coverage of Disney Parks are (space) mountains of minutiae that some fans only learned to care about because of WDW News Today. Corless, for example, was the first to introduce coverage of new park merchandise—which he credited as being "an important pillar of the business." Corless also devoted manpower to construction and food, the latter of which proved odd because of the nascent nature of his site's coverage.

"Snack reviews felt weird. It was odd for us to stand there photographing food for a half-hour before eating. We were grown men with expensive cameras shooting a cupcake all over Hollywood Boulevard," he said. "Now if you do that, no one even bats an eye. That's a very normal function of many of the fan sites."

Corless wasn't afraid to let his staff take chances on those or anything else, noting that topics like cupcake reviews might get 1,500 page views or 30,000 and predicting which way it would go was all but impossible. He said WDW News Today devoted time to dozens of podcasts and other ideas that never took off, including one devoted to movie reviews. But the eternally fickle nature of Disneyphiles meant nothing would ever be completely off the table.

"The most-read story on our site one year was when they were changing the flavors at Club Cool," he said of the 2013 soda swap at the former Epcot attraction. "I have a better idea now about what people want, but every once in a while I'm still surprised. Like with Ohana (at Disney's Polynesian Resort) removing their noodles (in favor of curry fried rice in early 2019). People went into an uproar the likes of which I've never seen."

Consumption of all things WDW News Today continued at a gluttonous pace through the second part of the decade. And he adapted throughout that time, altering the podcast schedule and anything else that needed tweaking. Once a top-10 travel show, the podcast has slowly simmered on the backburner while the focus shifted toward video. Corless set up a channel to post park and discussion shows, he live-streams broadcasts on all of his social media channels and in 2019 Corless bought a studio in Orlando to host a live weekly show in front of an audience that he said, at least prior to Covid-19, was "more popular than the podcast had ever been." This comprehensive approach gained Corless a lot of respect, both from park sources who were willing to confide in him and mainstream media who trusted his reporting enough to cite his scoops on stories such as the "Star Wars" hotel project at Walt Disney World and the breaking of ground for Mickey and Minnie's Runaway Railway at Disneyland. [4, 5] Of course, anyone who was near an internet-connected device in summer 2019 knows that reporting prowess can also occasionally get Corless in trouble. Corless, relying upon information from multiple sources, reported that the Magic Kingdom's Country Bear Jamboree would be replaced by a *Toy Story*-themed marionette show as part of Walt Disney World's 50th anniversary celebration in 1971. [6] That report was followed shortly after by another one stating the Magic Kingdom's Enchanted Tiki Room might be replaced by a *Moana*-themed show. [7] Disney took the extraordinary step of rebuking the reports—something that's rarely done by a megacorporation in regards to a blog post, at least in such a direct manner—due to the fashion with which the reports went viral. [8, 9]] Fans of the beloved if stale attractions made quick work of Corless, calling him a liar and plenty of other things that have no place to be reprinted in a family book. [10]

Relying upon his journalistic background, Corless said he and his team sat on the story for several weeks before publishing the story.

"We didn't know how they'd respond," Corless said of Disney. "That could look bad for us. Rumors (of park changes) are meant to be this fun thing. You as the reader can decide, 'Do I believe this or do I not?' That's just the function of fandom. Our decision ultimately was that we weren't quick enough to get people mobilized about the Great Movie Ride (Corless' site first reported on the attraction August 2017, 12 months prior). We felt the same thing could happen with Bears. We decided, 'Let's run early, and the company can see feedback from people.' After a week and a half, the company decided to say we were an unscrupulous source and we were trying to hurt the company. It honestly made us a lot stronger." [11]

Corless maintains that the story was solid and his team did the right thing by reporting the rumor. He accused the company's theme parks segment of being "petty" and noted that the company has denied attraction changes (such as shuttering California Adventure's Tower of Terror in favor of Guardians of the Galaxy—Mission: Breakout) only to later have to rescind those words.

Fact-checking has shown that Corless and his site have had some misses, among them a claim that Universal's Orlando property would close two of its Marvel-themed rides in 2015. And stories such as the "Star Wars"-themed hotel that WDW News Today claims to have broken may have been sourced from message boards or social media, according to analysis done by other sites. [12] But Corless has long stood by his reporting and did so again during the interview for this book, saying most content creators would like to have the proven results and accuracy that he does.

"Look at the rumors about sports restarting during the coronavirus thing. When that doesn't happen, people don't riot against ESPN. I don't think it always works. But Bears had traction because people know our track record. If it's put out by any other site, I don't think people would have bought into it. People knew if they read about it on our site, within a day or two it would be on the (Disney) Parks Blog. People obviously know when we post something, there's something there. We scooped even the Orange County Register on what the contents of the Marvel (Avengers Campus at Disneyland) would be. The big loss was within 48 hours, we lost 800 Twitter followers, but we recouped them in the four days following that. There were so many new people coming in. They'd say, 'I only found you because of the Country Bear thing.' "

Corless' work since his move to Orlando certainly qualifies as a success. The site, which is now his full-time work, draws 10 million pageviews a month across all of its operations. His reporters and photographers are all market-local—including one in Japan who covers Tokyo Disney—while other writers and show hosts are scattered about the United States. Once reliant upon Google for its advertising revenue, WDW News Today long ago grew large enough to draw other advertising clients who pay 10 times or more what Google generally does, although Corless did give Google credit for allowing his site to go full time to begin with.

The company, like many of its peers, has also branched out more generally into the Disney-related entertainment realm, including reporting in summer 2020 that Beyonce was negotiating to join the cast of Marvel's "Black Panther 2" and Disney+ projects. Such reporting diversifies the content (clearly an advantageous move during the coronavirus outbreak) while also attracting even more potential advertisers, Corless said.

This success has allowed WDW News Today to venture into the events business. Among them was a dessert party and walk-through the site hosted inside the Great Movie Ride just prior to its closure, which Corless called a career highlight. The process began after tickets sold out for a D23 "last call" event that the fan club ran in conjunction with American Movie Classics. Corless reached out to a contact in Disney's events department who began a weeks-long process to grant approval for the event—the first time any fan site has ever rented out a Disney attraction. Corless jumped through the hoops and got approval at 4:55 p.m. on a Friday to host the event seven days later. The $40,000 worth of tickets he needed to sell in order to pay for the event sold out within 48 hours; enough was left over to make a donation to CalArts in honor of Marty Sklar, the longtime Imagineer who died a month prior to the August 2017 event. [13] The 250 attendees, as best as Corless could tell, left satisfied.

"People were thanking my parents, who didn't even realize that I was really running a company until then. We'd been full time less than a year at that point. They were still waiting for me to come back to them saying I ran out of money," he said.

What Corless considers a perhaps even better event was one he hosted for the last day of IllumiNations at Epcot in September 2019. [14] Corless was able to piece together the creative team that'd created the nighttime attraction 20 years prior, part of a full day of presentations prior to a VIP viewing. It all began during an event he'd hosted that previous summer for the 30th anniversary of the Indiana Jones Stunt Spectacular at Hollywood Studios. While there, Corless ran into Ron Logan, a longtime Disney executive who worked in creative show development for the parks. [15] Logan gave quick approval of the idea Corless pitched for an IllumiNations show and offered a helping hand.

"He takes his Rolodex out of his bag. In it are all the names you've heard about. If they were part of the parks, they were in that thing," Corless said.

Among those names was Don Dorsey, a longtime production consultant who helped put together numerous Disney shows, including IllumiNations. [16] Corless had planned on calling Dorsey the following week, but before he could Dorsey called him offering his help. All it took was an agreement for Corless and his site to pay for a reunion dinner.

"The opportunity to put them all in a room was pretty amazing," Corless said. "I paid for dinner and handled ticket sales. I was willing to take a loss. I didn't care. I just thought it was going to be meaningful enough for people."

The event—which featured $300 packages—quickly sold out, putting any financial concerns to bed. Also part of the festivities were composer Gavin Greenway and vocalist Kellie Coffey, who together were part of the original IllumiNations composition. [17] The event further solidified the position of WDW News Today as an all-encompassing virtual location for Disneyphiles. He had big hopes for the studio show—which, even when charging people to attend, would draw 30 or more people a week—but the onset of coronavirus the subsequent Disney parks shutdown temporarily halted that production and many others for many other Disney podcasters, bloggers and vloggers. But WDW News Today didn't halt everything, maintaining regular posts and hosting at-home shows through the duration of the pandemic.

Indeed, the site expanded in June 2020 with the launch of Universal Parks News Today. The site claimed a high interest from its followers for Universal content even before the pandemic, but the dearth of news (along with the fact that Universal Studios Florida reopened more than a month before Walt Disney World) led to even more theme park-starved readers calling for coverage. It also gave the operation an additional revenue source that offered short-term relief during the Covid-19 recovery and nearly endless long-term opportunities. It launched with a dedicated URL, YouTube channel and social media channels.

"While WDWNT.com was founded to provide news and information about the Disney parks around the world, there has been a resounding demand by our audience to give them the same quality level and frequency of coverage for the Universal Orlando Resort," Corless wrote on the site. [18]

A continuing strong response from the site's fans had Corless hopeful that he and others in the Disney blogosphere could recover along with the economy going into 2021. Succeeding through tough times like that also solidified in him the fact that, even though the site and all of its peripheries were now a career, to a lot of people those properties were a lot more.

"How can you abandon people at this time? We wanted to still have that connection. It was about making money. It was the right thing to do," he said. "This was one of those rare events where the parks can't be there for you. After Sept. 11, the first thing we wanted to do was to get away. Disney was a place that made you feel home. Not having it during this time is rough. That's what we all know when we're not feeling good."

Sources:

1. https://livingbydisney.com/living-disney-media-kit
2. https://www.courant.com/os-cfb-talking-with-deb-willis-20160228-story.html
3. https://web.archive.org/web/20070715033344/http://www.wdwnewstoday.com/gpage.html
4. https://www.miamiherald.com/living/travel/article234303787.html
5. https://www.ocregister.com/2018/10/31/is-disneyland-getting-its-first-ride-based-on-mickey-mouse/
6. https://wdwnt.com/2019/06/rumor-disney-world-to-replace-country-bear-jamboree-with-toy-story-marionette-show-for-magic-kingdoms-50th-anniversary/
7. https://wdwnt.com/2019/06/rumor-walt-disneys-enchanted-tiki-room-will-be-replaced-with-a-moana-show-for-magic-kingdoms-50th-anniversary/
8. https://wdwnt.com/2019/06/breaking-disney-states-country-bear-jamboree-will-not-close-at-walt-disney-world/

9. https://wdwnt.com/2019/06/update-disney-denies-rumors-of-tiki-room-overlay-still-remains-silent-on-country-bear-jamboree/
10. https://monorailnews.com/2019/08/22/editorial-tom-corless-is-a-liar-who-doesnt-care-about-the-truth/
11. https://wdwnt.com/2016/08/rumor-the-great-mickey-ride-replacing-movie-ride-at-disneys-hollywood-studios/
12. https://www.orlando-rising.com/disney-world-fan-blog-says-its-at-war-with-the-company-it-covers/
13. https://disneyparks.disney.go.com/blog/2017/07/legendary-disney-imagineer-marty-sklar-dies-at-83/
14. https://touringplans.com/epcot/attractions/illuminations-reflections-of-earth
15. https://d23.com/walt-disney-legend/ron-logan
16. http://www.dondorseyconsulting.com/dd/dd_home.htm
17. https://wdwnt.com/2019/09/video-say-goodbye-to-illuminations-with-a-live-performance-of-promise-by-vocalist-kellie-coffey-and-composer-gavin-greenway
18. https://wdwnt.com/2020/06/wdwnt-embarks-on-epic-expansion-with-launch-of-universal-parks-news-today/

CHAPTER FIVE

Believing All the Way, Implicitly and Unquestionably

Raise your hand if you grew up dreaming of running a successful Disney YouTube channel.

Yep, didn't think so.

While there might be a few people born in the 21st century who grew up dreaming about being a Disney content creator, that wasn't exactly up there with fireman, princess or velociraptor wrangler when the creators featured in this text were young. One thread that runs through them all, including the stories you've already read about in this text: Their current content-creation operations in no way resemble what they pictured would come to pass when they got started.

"If you want to make God laugh," Hill said with a chuckle, "make a plan."

Indeed, planning on hitting it big in blogging or podcasting pretty much ranks up there with planning to settle on Mars or expecting a Disney movie character's parents to live through the entire film in terms of far-fetched ideas. As such, many members of the internet Disneysphere participate more so for pleasure that for business. Even the most successful Disney and theme park-related products don't drive truly titanic traffic, with true-crime and celebrity-hosted podcasts consistently topping the Chartable top 200; no Disney-related show made that list, with WDW Radio and Be Our Guest among the very few to make any of Chartable's sublists (both have been in the top 100 for some foreign nation's places and travel specialty podcast lists). Emerging as an internet success is almost a statistical anomaly; 69 percent of all bloggers make no money at all, with only 2 percent across all topics earning over $150,000 from their work. [1]

There also has to be some degree of perseverance woven into the fabric of any creation, though. More than one out of every 10 podcasts does not even publish a second episode, according to podcast agency Pacific Content. Half of all shows that are started have 14 or fewer episodes. The most-played shows tend to have catalogs well into the triple-digits, meaning creators tend to have to stick with it for years in order to bear significant fruit. [2]

Jerusha Tano-Fett of the now-defunct Disney Chef, which recreated favorite Disney theme park dishes, put in between 35 and 60 hours a week on her blog for several years starting in 2012. From organizing content to studying algorithms and updating recipes, there was more than a full plate in front of her at all times. She also shared that running a site changed the way she vacationed, which is something may prospective content creators might not consider: "On one hand, I know a lot of the cool tips, tricks, hidden tidbits, and other sly little ways to make the most of my time at Disney. On the other, vacations often feel like working vacations. I'm always taking notes, stopping for pictures, and thinking of how to share what I'm experiencing with my readers. Literally nobody in my family remembers what it's like to eat a meal at Disney without me standing over their shoulder and getting pictures first." She cautioned to temper expectations, but with enough elbow grease (or finger joint grease, or whatever) success could be had. [3]

It's not about the fame or fortune, of course. They might disappoint Yoda, but may creators would say the adventure and excitement that comes with their projects are the main cravings they have. Some work for years just to be able to break even on their projects, making a little bit of money to cover production expenses. Some are not even that fortunate. But that's generally not a deterrent, as running a blog or podcast is more about the message that's being shared than the profitability of said thought.

"I've had some amazing times, shared experiences being down there," Yaglenski said. "Our sites have been the gateway to that."

A remote communications and PR professional living in South Carolina, Yaglenski does have regrets about not trying to pursue the site full time—but he has no regrets about where his money did go. Aside from covering equipment, server and other costs, money generated from InterCOT was often used to host get-togethers at Walt Disney World for the site's users. They began in the early 2000s when, as he put it, the concept of meeting people from the internet was usually responded to with something along the lines of "I hope you don't get murdered." And every trip has more than paid for itself with memories. The first trip saw one of the roughly 100 Intercot fans who were in the audience of Who Wants to Be a Millionaire—Play It! At the former Disney-MGM Studios. She told the host that she was there with a bunch of people she'd met on the internet, and the audience response was the sort of bewilderment generally reserved for people trying to understand what the thinking was behind letting "Planes: Fire & Rescue" be made.

In another get-together, he'd secured a VIP seating area near the United Kingdom pavilion at Epcot for IllumiNations. The party had started near the Norway pavilion, with blue glow-stick lanyards among the goodies. Yaglenski went over early to get the area arranged, and closer to show time he saw this swarm of blue light make its way from Norway through China and Germany toward him (one of the few times that a swarm of people marching out of Germany produced anything positive).

"It was one of the most surreal things. Knowing that these were all my people—I was like the dad, and these were my kids. It was one of those 'This is what I built' moments," he said.

For others, creating a Disney-related site has helped honor what their forefathers built. Among the many accomplishments of Frost's grandfather was to have a key role in the construction of the Haunted Mansion; Vic Greene's name was actually on the attraction's original blueprints as a head architect. But, as Frost tells it, Greene's wife was upset that Victor had a tombstone put up in his honor (using only his first name, Victor) at the Disneyland version of the attraction, considering it "flippant." So, after having removed all of the tombstones in 1970 to expand the ride queue, Disneyland honored her wishes and didn't include Victor's tombstone among those it put back up during a 1973 relocation. [4]

In 2014, Frost—through The Disney Blog—organized a petition to have the tombstone put back or some other acknowledgement of his grandfather's work put into place at the attraction. [5] Two years later, the tombstones of Victor and a dozen other people were restored. [6]

"To me, that's amazingly cool. That was the park where he got started," Frost said. "It's nice he gets his credit back—a little bit of magic that was made just because."

The fruits of many content creators' labors aren't quite that bountiful, but they're no less sweet for those making them. Jeff DePaoli has been harvesting fruit since February 2014 in the form of Dizney Coast to Coast, a podcast that has featured pretty much a weekly look at the wonderful world of Disney in the form of interviews, reviews and special segments such as Princess Pondering, which delves into the history of a different Disney princess episode.

A Massachusetts native, DePaoli got into Disney and show business as a child, first falling in love with "The Little Mermaid." That interested was cemented in the handprints outside of the replica Grauman's Chinese Theatre when he first visited Walt Disney World in November 1989. In a phone interview, he said that was his first real introduction to movies and Disneyana. He delved into both interests more through his teens and used his performing arts degree to break into that world when he moved to the Los Angeles area in September 2006—a cross-country road that included a stop in Marcelline. He got various entertainment-related jobs, including making a mark as a "scratcher" during Halloween Horror Nights at Universal Studios Hollywood and as a Warner Bros. studio tour guide. He also delved into a variety of side projects, including a one-man show he created in Boston that was rebooted in Los Angeles and appearing on a '90s-related podcast that a friend started. The content, including the "Honey I Shrunk the Kids" franchise, Rosie O'Donnell and "Newsies" is well-known by Coast to Coast listeners to be squarely in DePaoli's wheelhouse.

"I went on that show and had a good time, and at the end he said, 'You need to have your own podcast.

You just have to.' I said, 'Do I?' I don't know how," DePaoli said.

Months more of cajoling convinced DePaoli to give a Disney-themed show a whirl, after giving some thought to what an original concept could be in an already-crowded field. He and partner Patrick Dougall together launched Coast to Coast—so-named because Dougall lived in Florida—to give Disney fans a range of entertaining options from interviews to event previews and specialty shows like Princess Pondering, detailing the history of a different Disney princess each episode. Dougall left after about a year, but DePaoli is still going strong. He's had a range of guests and perks over the years, but for DePaoli the best memories come from getting to know the people and stories behind the scenes.

"I am weird about celebrity stuff. I could be standing next to Johnny Depp and I honestly wouldn't care," he said. "Celebrity doesn't excite me. I nerd out around producers and stuff. I love people who create things. (Producer) David Kirschner of 'Hocus Pocus,' that blows my mind that he's my friend (he was a guest on the show in July 2018)."

Heaton has a similar motivation in running Tomorrow Society. Most his memorable moments with his entry in the Disneysphere involve people whose names aren't familiar but work most definitely is. Some of his standout episodes involved talking to composer Bruce Broughton, who's scored Disney movies such as "The Rescuers Down Under" as well as attractions like Spaceship Earth and Ellen's Energy Adventure; Rick Harper, who directed the "Impressions de France" film at the Epcot France pavilion, and Peggie Fariss, a former Imagineer who could count Spaceship Earth among a half-century's worth of credits.

"To be able to talk to someone whose story isn't as well know—in some way, I felt like there is something else here. I want to make sure that my guests who are taking the time to do this, that they're able to tell their stories. This is a really interesting person who's had a really great career," said Heaton, who graduated from the journalism program at the University of Missouri.

Heaton hopes that, in his own small way, he can inspire his readers and listeners the way that he was inspired by the people he's introducing to his audience.

"Almost everyone got to Disney in kind of a weird way. Most didn't say they were going to be an Imagineer at age 8 and got there. There's always crazy stories. The origin stories are always so interesting. There's an audience for that among a certain type of person like me, people who have the Disney gene," he said.

Hill contends that, while his work with his company Jim Hill Media is enough to sustain him, the biggest payment comes in the form of learning 30 years' worth of good backstage stories. Among the highlights is the story of David Mumford, an Imagineer who died in January 2003 due to non-Hodgkin's lymphoma. [7] In speaking to Mumford once upon a time, Hill said the two of them fondly recalled the "Disney Goes to the Fair" episode of "The Wonderful World of Color" and seeing robotic dinosaurs eating. As Hill recalls, Mumford said something along the lines of, "Imagineers got paid to build giant robotic dinosaurs, which is how I knew that I had to become an Imagineer." Mumford ultimately got a job as an Imagineer as part of a 3,000-plus hiring surge when the company was ramping up production to build Epcot. He was assigned, for his first job, to make the animatronic brontosaurus that appeared in the original Universe of Energy attraction. Hill remembers Mumford being a bit teary-eyed: "Why are you crying?

He replied, 'I just achieved a childhood dream, don't mind me.' "

Then there's the accident that became the Epcot International Flower & Garden Festival. Hill said his research found that the idea began in 1994, when CommuniCore was shuttered in favor of Innoventions. While that area went behind construction fences for the winter and spring, park administrators had to put in something to entertain guests.

"Flowers are cheap," Hill said they came to realize. "It served as basically a distraction."

But the following year, there was enough demand for Disney to return the flowers to Epcot. Thus, an inadvertent tradition was born.

As priceless as stories like this might be, none of this is to say that there's a complete absence of money changing hands. Heaton hosts a Patreon on his site, with donors getting access to exclusive content such as his exhaustive scene-by-scene account of Spaceship Earth. Yaglenski still brings in a fair amount of ad revenue, even if the total doesn't match what it once did; he said it's enough for him to "treat my moderators well" while paying for the site's hosting and upkeep. The triumvirate at Enchanted Tiki Talk sell enough sponsorships to cover a handful of expenses.

"Could we get more money? Probably. But that's not our real goal," Duffy said. "As long as we're not paying for it ourselves, it's not that expensive. But say you spend $200 a year on hosting. You have to buy a mic and other equipment. It's just nice to have a little bit of money."

Frost was once making enough money to consider turning Disney Blog into a full-time venture, but he preferred that the site allowed him to sharpen his skills for his day job as a digital and social media marketer. Matt Parrish sold T-shirts and theme park-based candles through his wife's soy-based candle company, along with selling a couple sponsorships that were enough to host a scaled-down show.

DePaoli, who also runs a Patreon and sells calendars and other merchandise, hopes that content consumers realize that most creators have full-time jobs not involving their sites, and that their side hustles involve a lot more hustle than honey. He has parlayed his site into other ventures, such as serving as the voice of Disney Trivia on Amazon Echo Dot Kids Edition, but he feels creators need more support from their audiences to give enough of an incentive to keep creating.

"Audience members feel entitled to free content. But it's not really free. Use affiliate links. The reality is all of these things are going to go away eventually if they're not making money," he said. "Everybody wants everything for free, but you don't get Disney+ for free. People think things should always be free unless, ironically, it comes from a giant corporation that needs the money less than a smaller operation would—the people that are probably taking a huge-ass risk that you're not aware of."

Mongello concurs, noting that most consumers don't realize the hours upon hours of preparation and thought that go into every word typed or said: "There's no shortcuts. You can't buy a shortcut. It takes time. We're in this age of instant gratification. It's very much a marathon, not a sprint. You have to keep pushing the finish line farther away."

Some revel in the pursuit of the next goal. Others grow tired of a never-ending run and move on. A lucky few stumble across something magical—living the dream of one's work not really being work. DePaoli stressed that the experiences have more than made his time on Dizney Coast to Coast worth the effort.

That sentiment is unanimously agreed upon by anyone who's ever fired up a keyboard or microphone.

"To me, if it led to something financial, that's great. But if you go into this thinking this is your money-maker, you're not going to do it for very long. Even people that have been successful, they did it for years for no money or they did it for years and it hit," DePaoli said.

Nikida Vaughn said she hopes the eight-plus years of perseverance she's shown with her site Theme Park Hipster lead to something more, and that she can in time run the site and author books full-time: "I just love it, and I look at it as freedom. I don't see myself as being a pharmacist forever ... It's that freedom that I see, and not just freedom that I can wake up anytime I want but the freedom that I can spend time with my family when I need to. I have a passion for that feeling you have when you get there and you're just escaping."

Frost, meanwhile, is content to have The Disney Blog fund his Disney habit, including annual passes and the occasional hotel stay. He moved to Florida in 2005 from Las Vegas after the dot-com crash sank their fortunes and those of many others (he and his wife wanted to be near one of the Disney parks, he said, and "we didn't like the traffic of California, neither of us spoke Japanese and our French is pretty rusty, so Florida it was)." But he never aspired to make the blog his career. He writes 2-3 hours a night and another few hours over the weekend, with guest writers filling in the gaps.

"I never really focused on monetizing it," he said. "To me, this is a passion project. I enjoy the amount of time I have to put into it for the most part, but I don't want it to be a full-time job."

Anyone looking to break into the Disneysphere as a contributor better have the same inkling. One analysis that was published by Theme Park Tribune found that Disney-related pieces totaling 3,000 words (about 7 percent of the length of this book) for an unverified website paid the less-than-hearty sum of $6 (probably a good portion of the net proceeds of this book). Other sites that were analyzed paid a fraction more, with Chip and Co. paying about 1.2 cents per word and Inside the Magic paying on a per-click scale that tends to average around 5 cents per work (with the potential for much more). Corless' WDW News Today paid $12 per story for contributors and at least $12 per hour for its hourly workers. [8] Some sites welcome contributions in exchange for the "experience" of being published online—a model that's worked well for years for the likes of Huffington Post.

For the Parrish brothers, WEDway Radio and the Disneysphere allowed them to maintain connections they'd been forging for years. They'd been making trips since the 1980s with their family, and both Nate (Sci-Fi Drive-In) and their sister (Liberty Tree Tavern) got jobs there as part of the Disney College Program. Matt lost touch with his Disney gene for a bit after that, but Nate got big on Disney history right around the time that podcasts first became a thing in the early 2000s. Matt reconnected with the Mouse House after a bit, looping Disney background music to help pass the time while he worked as an overnight radio broadcaster.

The brothers further forged their Disney bonds through an email game they played (texting wasn't a thing—or a word— yet) in which one of them would give three clues, and the other would have to guess which attraction was being thought of. The game reinforced their park knowledge and made them both want to learn more about what went into attraction development. That game, combined with trips the brothers took with their respective spouses in the first part of the 2000s, convinced the Parrishes to launch their show in 2009. Matt said the show was meant to satiate Disney nerds like him and his brother who couldn't get enough about Disney history.

"When you first start doing something like that, you're really into it. You have a lot of passion and ideas," Matt Parrish said. "The shows allow you to connect with people in ways you didn't imagine. After a couple years and getting a listener base, you develop relationships through that. Sometimes they're superficial, but sometimes they're very in-depth. And it's sometimes the way that the relationships form. 'I had cancer for six months and I was in the hospital bed, and your show pulled me through'—those are the types of emails we would get."

The podcast eventually took a backseat for Nate—"Life gets in the way," as Matt put it—so Matt shifted focus in recent years to a different show. He and Kevin Quickey are into their fourth season of The Thirty20Eight, which focuses on the history and "listory" of the Disney parks. Matt got to know Quickey when the latter guest-hosted on WEDWay Radio 17 tiimes in 2016; they then launched The Thirty20Eight, Matt's self-described WEDWay Radio spin-off show, in February 2017.

Both shows have helped satisfy Matt's desire for deep dives into Disney history. As the surge this century in comic cons and related events has proven, he said, the public's appetite for such content has continued to grow almost faster than he and related outlets can create it.

"The topics are endless. Design theory, attractions, important people. There's so many different ways to talk about Disney because it's such a multifaceted conglomerate," he said. "D23 expos—they've provided a brand new avenue for these Disney primary sources to come out and share their stories. Bill Farmer at D23, he had a packed crowd. Twenty-five years ago, Bill Farmer doesn't have that. It's really a tremendous thing to let these people share their stories."

Farmer has also made the rounds within the Disneysphere, appearing on shows like Enchanted Tiki Talk along with fellow Disney Legends like Rollie Crump and Bob Gurr.

"Farmer was such a nice guy just to make the time for three dudes who were five or six episodes into a show that had a very small following," Brown said. "Rollie Crump, the stories he had—it was truly like sitting down with Walt Disney."

While very few people who are still with us know what it was like to sit down with Walt, the feeling his work was able to convey is ubiquitous to anyone who's been fortunate enough to experience it. To rekindle that flame, both for themselves and for the followers, is worth as much or more than any financial compensation that their work could conceivably create.

"I never would have imagined that this was someone's safe space when commuting to work. Maybe there's other people at your workplace that don't really get it. The podcast allows you to connect with people who get it," Parrish said.

In addition to enriching the souls of Disney fans, some content creators are looking to up their followers' fashion games. The Walt Disney Company has ramped up its merchandise offerings over the past decade, and segments of the Disneysphere have honed in to help users look their best. Content creators like Chelsea Watson (@StyledByMagic on Instagram) like to showcase outfits that can let a Disneyphile proclaim their fandom yet not look entirely out of place when at home or elsewhere.

"I really like showcasing clothing that, if you took away the ears, you would still be comfortable wearing it outside the park," she told Bustle. [9]

Her 70,000-plus followers get her insights on the parks and the looks that the parks inspire—usually accompanied by some sort of mouse ear-like headgear. Other creators like Leslie Kay (who likes to imagine what Disney characters might look like in the real world in everyday clothing) and Magic by Muses (who have a knack for finding an outfit to match most any Disneyland setting) look to offer a little couture creativity.

Some people even use the blogosphere to vent about Disney. Paige Wolf posted a "Top 10 Reasons I Hated Disney World" blog entry that took off for (and generally not in a good way, judging by the backlash she said she encountered across the internet). Some of her complaints—an unbalanced diet at the parks, unruly children melting down in the heat, incomplete or not-thought-out attractions and lands, and too much overpriced merchandise—might be valid. But the pushback produced by the post compelled her to write a follow-up, showing that there is no shortage of space for debate within the Disneysphere. [10]

Of course, more people will pursue a project out of passion than out of spite. Whatever niche part of the Disney culture draws your interest, Frost said anyone with a love of something relating to the company should pursue it. He estimates that he's had about 50 different contributors to his site over the years, each of whom was given a chance to develop their voice and hone their strengths while pursuing a dream; some of them have gone on to work for the Walt Disney Company.

Those who are most successful keep a handful of key points in mind:

- Figure out what their "why" is and stick to it; without some sort of focus, fans won't know what to expect when they come to you.
- Determine a target audience.
- Stay consistent with activity, even if traffic doesn't come for weeks ... or months ... or years.
- Find a need and attempt to meet that need.
- If you lose passion for what you're doing, then it might be time to move on; the work that's needed to endure through the blog-building process can't be understated, and without loving it you won't make it through the tough days—and there will be tough days.

"I hope the blog community continues to grow. I would encourage people to find what they're passionate about and write about it online—movies, parks, pins. It takes five minutes to start a blog, and it's free," said Frost, who noted that he maintains an open line of communication with anyone who's looking for advice or feedback on their work. "That's part of my goal as a Disney blogger is to find other Disney fans and help them find their passion."

Sources:

1. https://99firms.com/blog/blogging-statistics/#gref
2. https://blog.pacific-content.com/podcast-success-a-long-game-fd6522b72752
3. http://www.thedisneychef.com/2014/03/full-time-disney-blogger.html
4. https://hauntedmansion.fandom.com/wiki/Victor
5. https://thedisneyblog.com/2014/10/16/petition-to-return-a-lost-tombstone-to-the-haunted-mansion/
6. https://thedisneyblog.com/2016/09/12/disneyland-restores-tribute-tombstones-haunted-mansion/

7. http://jimhillmedia.com/editor_in_chief1/b/jim_hill/archive/2003/01/22/222.aspx
8. https://www.themeparktribune.com/popular-disney-blogs-pay-writers-as-little-as-3-per-article/
9. https://www.bustle.com/p/inside-the-fantastical-world-of-disney-fashion-bloggers-8201725
10. https://spitthatoutthebook.com/2016/01/top-10-reasons-i-hated-disney-world/

CHAPTER SIX

Curiosity, Confidence, Courage, Constancy

Disney is a passion and a hobby for plenty of people, but only a select few have gotten to combine business with pleasure and make covering the parks a profession. But as the number of people trying to so grows, the volume of potential clients and customers grows at a faster rate. The number of people attending Walt Disney World's parks continues to surge even as admission costs consistently, annoyingly creep upward. The four parks drew a combined 58.31 million visitors in 2018, up from 55.87 million the year before (an increase of 4.2 percent) and from 48.5 million in 2012 (an increase of 16.82 percent). [1] The one-day ticket cost increased from $89 to $109, indicating that people are willing to pay for what they want from their theme park. Disney theme parks worldwide saw 157.31 million visitors in 2018, more than three times the number of people (50.07 million) who visited Universal attractions. Those visitors put $12.92 billion into the bank accounts of Walt Disney Company shareholders. [2] The company also boasted 52.54 million Facebook followers, 6.7 million Twitter followers and 25.1 million Instagram followers as of June 2020. While not in the top 10 on any of those platforms—such rarefied air is reserved for uber-celebs like Cristiano Ronaldo and Dwayne Johnson on the individual level, and Samsung, Coca-Cola and McDonald's on the brand level—those are still lofty numbers that indicate great interest in what the Mouse House is doing.

And Disney customers come back at a rate most other businesses would envy. Around 70 percent of first-time Disney customers come back for seconds—and often thirds, fourth and twenty-fifths. [3] So a content creator finding the right way to connect with his or her audience could easily make a fan for life.

New York University professor David Forgacs issued an academic report based around the notion that Americans are literally born into a love of Disney, and only by external circumstances are they weened away from the company. While his "Disney Animation and the Business of Childhood" was written before anyone had registered even an AOL account, his 1992 paper theorized that the term "Disney Baby" refers to anyone born after 1925, two years after Walt and Roy Disney founded their cartoon studio. Anyone born after that timeframe, the author contends, couldn't help but see Disney films in the theaters, read Disney books and comics, and own some sort of Disney paraphernalia in their youth. Those children who were captivated by first runs of *Snow White and the Seven Dwarfs* have become grandparents of *Frozen* fans and Pixar pushers, almost etching Disney into part of the American fabric itself. The theme parks serve to further cultivate the next generation of Disney fans while appealing to the nostalgic notions of their parents, he wrote: "Children are a major source of Disney income, but only indirectly: It is adults who spend money on them." [4]

So if this continually growing section of the population is going to spend money on Disney and the parks, it only makes sense that some people within that group try to capitalize and make a living while also living a dream and helping others relive theirs. And that often results in people moving south to be closer to where the magic happens.

In Matt Roseboom's case, the move was north, and he made a mainstay among the Orlando theme park circuit by simultaneously bucking the online trend and embracing how the internet could deliver news. In a phone interview, he said he owned a couple newspapers in southwest Florida at the turn of the 21st century. Frequent visitors to the theme park—he moved to South Florida as an adult, having grown up in Ohio and visited Cedar Point and other parks there in his childhood—he said he had considered devoting his career to Walt Disney World for a while, but when he sold his newspapers in 2007 the sale came with a no-compete clause so he was in need of new employment.

So he and his family drove up to Orlando and launched Attractions Magazine with partner Ricky Brigante. Roseboom bought Brigante out inside of a year, but as part of the transaction he took with him a side project he'd created, Inside the Magic —one of the internet's longest-running podcasts (Roseboom said the split was in part because there wouldn't be enough money for both of them to own it, while Brigante cited a difference in visions). [5] A background in web media management (Roseboom was the web manager for the Marco Island Eagle and New York Times in the late-1990s) gave him the experience and realization that he needed a solid online presence, but given that he's a print journalist at heart he also wanted to build a traditional product.

Roseboom saw an advantage to diversifying the places he covered, so he opted to make his publication one of few to cover all of the parks in central Florida—not just Walt Disney World and Universal Studios but also Sea World, Legoland and other secondary sites.

That helped him find a small but underserved customer base, he said, while gaining him access to parks that might sometimes get lost in the never-ending cyclone of Disney and Universal coverage. It also earned him accolades (the Orlando Sentinel named Attractions its best theme park/tourism blog in 2009) and precious shelf space, with the magazine earning spots in Barnes & Nobles and Borders stores nationwide within a couple years of launch. [6]

That gave him a big leg up on his competitors—a field that was relatively light compared to today but still a lot bigger than a decade prior. But he knew he had to stand out even more in order to maximize his business' potential.

Roseboom was also perhaps the Tay Zonday of the Disneysphere, branching out onto YouTube before a lot of people understood what exactly that was. The reasoning was organic: "We realized we were covering all of these events with all this hoopla going on, so we should record it." Videos from all of those parks, along with live podcast recordings and other specials, helped the YouTube channel top 700,000 subscribers in relatively short order. [7] A cornerstone of the YouTube channel was "Orlando Attractions Magazine—The Show," a regular roundup of theme park happenings. That grew a large enough following that it was picked up by Florida's Bright House Networks (now part of the Comcast/Spectrum family) as an on-demand offering to its subscribers. [8]

So the fame was cultivated in relatively quick fashion, but the fortune was much slower in coming.

"You don't make a bunch of money at the beginning," said Roseboom, who said he quickly realized he needed to diversify in order to thrive. "Our YouTube channel was going off really well right from the beginning (in August 2007)."

But the first few months were lean. Roseboom credits having a traditional print product and a freelancer who'd built credibility with the Walt Disney Company (who was able to get Attractions access it otherwise might not gain as a fledgling product) for helping it eventually break through.

"It was kind of a Catch-22. We would reach out to Disney for story requests, and they said to come back when you've been around for a year. Well, we're not going to be around for a year if you don't help us get access for these stories," said Roseboom, who noted that while pioneers like Frost and Yaglenski has given internet journalists some credibility, widespread access and acceptance hadn't been achieved in the mid-2000s. "The journalism background helps a lot. Anyone can start a blog and say they cover theme parks. But it takes a while to build up that trustworthiness. We clearly label rumors as rumors. People now who are starting websites may do what they have to do to get clicks on their websites. But people know if we say something, it's true."

That's helped Attractions build up its reputation as a public service. Visit Florida, the official tourism agency for the state, plugs Attractions as an official vacation planning device. [9] It also caught the eye of others within the Disney blogosphere; allears.net, for one, called it a "fun read" and a fitting replacement for Disney Magazine, which the Walt Disney Company ceased printing in 2005. [10] Chip & Company, meanwhile, said a subscription was a must for anyone looking to recapture Disney magic at home. [11]

Hearing from multi-generational Disney families brings Roseboom just as much, if not more, satisfaction than any accolades. He said his goal through Attractions is to help people recapture the magic they may have left behind when they flew back home out of

MCO: "It's a lot of the parents growing up going to the parks and experiencing these things, so they take their kids and now the kids are getting older. It's a family thing. With everything scary in the world, it's nice to get a little escape. When you're at one of the theme parks, you can kind of let those troubles go away."

Attractions also covers other amusement parks nationwide, creating a need for Roseboom to branch out—and to drop the word "Orlando" from the publication's name in 2014. He has a handful of freelancers in the Los Angeles area to cover Disneyland, and others scattered across the country to periodically cover major events in other areas. There's also a cadre of freelance writers, videographers and podcast hosts to help Roseboom, his wife, son and two other full-time workers put the product out. Top-tier subscriptions come with archive access and mystery merchandise boxes.

The quarterly magazine (it used to be printed bi-monthly) has a relatively small but loyal subscriber base of about 2,000, Roseboom said—enough to pay for itself and give the enterprise a center around which to revolve. That number has stayed fairly steady over the years, which Roseboom said is a credit to his readers in an age when print is going the way of Stitch's Great Escape. Just as importantly, Roseboom thinks the print magazine gives something for members of all generations to connect to.

"It's a lot of the parents grew up going to these parks and experiencing these things, so they take their kids and now their kids are getting older. It becomes a family thing," he said. "With everything scary in the world, it's nice to get a little escape. The website, magazine, videos, they let people experience a little bit of that from their homes."

Roseboom is hands-on throughout the process. He handles story editing, coverage assignments and overseeing social media, and he's still seen at park events from time to time. He also tries to crack the code of what will break through next. Attractions has had its fair share of hits (a series about park foods) and misses (daily vlogs with rotating hosts) but isn't afraid to try new things—mostly because he has to.

"There's no rhyme or reason as to why one video takes off and one doesn't. One of our competitors can post a video and get 50,000 views, and our video of the same thing might get only 5,000 views. The frustration comes in just trying to figure out that formula that changes all the time," said Roseboom, who noted that the trend in recent years has been to draw YouTube views from people who've never visited the parks and say they're living vicariously through the videos until they save up enough money for an in-person visit.

Also big for Attractions have been ride-through videos. Among its first videos were glances at the former Muppet Mobile Lab and what was then a new "O' Canada" video featuring Martin Short at the Canada Epcot pavilion. Fans have continued to flock to videos like that, he said, as well as more recent ride-through videos for Rise of the Resistance. One fan he met at that opening in late-2019 said she used Attractions' videos to gauge whether her autistic son could handle getting on the ride in person.

"He watched the video over and over again to build up confidence to ride it. He hated unexpected things, but that helped him get ready for it. She couldn't believe he rode it, and he loved it," he said.

That hasn't stopped advertisers from flocking to Attractions' various outlets, though. Roseboom said he brings in revenue from advertisers that specifically want to be featured on Attractions' various social media channels and the print magazine, which also has a digital version. All in all, the business is making enough money to allow the 50-year-old Roseboom to make a career out of it for as long as he likes—which could be for a while still.

"My business is always for sale for the right price, but that price is pretty high because I just enjoy what I do. My family enjoys it. It stays exciting for me. I don't want to do it forever. The goal is to get to a point where I have enough staff where they can do it day to day—sort of a semi-retirement," he said. "I'm purposely not covering city council meetings anymore. I'm covering fun things. We mix a lot of business and pleasure."

Sources:

1. https://www.bizjournals.com/orlando/datacenter/lists
2. https://www.statista.com/statistics/194323/attendance-figures-of-amusement-park-chains-worldwide-since-2010/
3. https://www.helpscout.com/blog/disney-customer-experience/
4. https://academic.oup.com/screen/article-abstract/33/4/361/1607047?redirectedFrom=PDF
5. https://insidethemagic.net/2018/03/itm-editor-founder-goodbye-see-ya-real-soon/
6. https://www.prweb.com/releases/2010/05/prweb3976934.htm
7. https://www.youtube.com/attractionsmagazine
8. https://www.attractiontickets.com/en/forum/showthread.php?13860-Orlando-Attractions-Magazine-The-Show-Now-Available-on-TV!
9. https://www.visitflorida.com/en-us/listing.a0t40000007qvcWAAQ.html
10. https://allears.net/2008/03/25/orlando-attractions-magazine-a-review
11. https://chipandco.com/one-more-disney-thing-you-cant-live-without-orlando-attractions-magazine-19524

CHAPTER SEVEN

Take Your Frown, Turn It Upside Down, and You'll Find Yours

The best kind of happiness is shared happiness. Just as Disney content creators look to help their consumers relive their best vacation moments, those who are lucky enough to do so take pride in being able to give people like them a little boost. Creating a content site large enough to support a full-time staff isn't impossible, but it takes a whole lot more than a spoonful of sugar and a wish upon a star to make it happen. It takes skill, certainly, but also fortunate timing, a little foresight and a good amount of luck.

Laughing Place has created many safe spaces in its more than two decades of operation. It's also created a pretty unique situation for Kyle Burbank, who after a break at the first D23 expo caught on as a site contributor and ended up becoming its full-time editorial director.

Burbank doesn't take his position of rarefied air—working full-time covering Disney without having launched a site of his own—lightly. At that first D23 in 2009, Burbank ran into a friend of the Moseleys who put in a good word for him. That got Burbank, who was living in California at the time, through the door periodically covering events for the site.

That site had already built quite the reputation. It launched in 1999 as "Your Entrance to Disneyland on the Web" and was among the first sites to feature food and entertainment highlights (along with midi sound files), merchandise and specific attraction write-ups. [1] It actually wasn't even Doobie Moseley's (real first name Eugene) first foray into the Disneysphere; he launched The Hub a year prior as a tribute to his happy place, a place he'd visited several times per year since his childhood in southern California. A computer programmer by trade, he set up the site to host his periodic columns, tributes, trivia and other park-related tidbits. [2] Rebekah, meanwhile, was an annual passholder for nearly a decade by that point and had her own tribute site to Disneyland ragtime pianist Rod Miller. [3]

The Moseleys quickly outgrew those projects, though, and set up Laughing Place to chronicle everything about the parks in Florida and California, as well as Disney media and collectibles. Frost was among a menagerie of columnists and contributors they had under their umbrella discussing park updates, improvements to Disney's own web properties and company history. It also offered Disney-related clip art and fan faction, as well as trip reports and people profiles.

The site continued to expand, launching one of the first Disney-related podcasts in the first part of the 2010s. Burbank added his expertise and helped build out a crew of a handful of full-time employees, including his wife R.D. Burbank, who serves as the news desk manager and site manager. Laughing Place continued to build its credentials over the years, becoming a go-to source for mainstream outlets like Variety when they needed Disney information.

"Those sorts of things kind of show our success," said Burbank, who noted that Laughing Place often tries to take a big-picture viewpoint on stories. "There's other sites that are good at being first, and they're on the scene all the time. If we're not first, then we think it's just better to take a breath and wait until we have more information. Our team is spread out more around the entire nation."

That includes the inexplicable Disney hotbed of Missouri. The Burbanks also call The Show-Me State home, making their headquarters in Springfield and managing a team that's sprinkled in most corners of the country. Burbank sometimes posts and directs all editorial staffers on what should be covered and how. Under his watch, the site focuses largely on day-to-day coverage, maintaining a running list of stories they want to get to in the shorter term. Ownership also remains involved. Doobie Moseley uses his developing skills to create internal programs that enhance the site's offerings.

As internet pioneers of sorts, the Moseleys have been open to trying most anything that's come about over the years—albeit with a bit of a learning curve. Laughing Place was an early adopter of video, but Burbank said that since no one there knew much about video editing they'd simply post entire raw videos. The site has since built up a sizable YouTube following, with an interview with Bob Chapek gaining decent traction with it was first posted but gaining a much better foothold nearly a year later when Chapek was named Disney's CEO. That channel has generated some revenue and is part of a diversification of income that Burbank said is beneficial to the operation (other sources include Google AdSense, sponsorships and an affiliation arrangement with Disney+). But it also brings its share of headaches, such as videos being pulled because some of the background parade music is copyrighted. Laughing Place also operates a popular Instagram account, which Burbank said was belatedly launched after realizing that their job involves covering "the most Instagrammed place on Earth," and its reviews of Disney+ programming and other Disney productions also draw wide audiences.

Burbank said there isn't much that's off the table. The site keeps a continually running account of attraction wait times, and it offers park recipes and guides to every Disney property on the globe. It's part of an effort to creatively keep people engaged without resorting to cheap tactics, Burbank said.

"We want to make people feel like once they've arrived (on the site), they have found something valuable, and we're not just tricking them to visit a different page and get a couple extra cents," he said.

The best way to meet that goal, he contends, is through the editorial product, which doesn't necessarily entirely avoid opinion but tries to play it down the middle as much as possible. Part of his mission is to offer context to the coverage so that fans can understand what's being discussed and why certain decisions are being made.

As for making coverage decisions, Burbank largely operates the site under the premise that if a story hasn't risen to the top of the list within a few days, it should either be reworked or dropped. He's also had a good deal of input on other aspects of the business—and he's thankful to the Moseleys that they respect his work and his opinion.

"The site had a very old design when I first started. For this site in particular, I really liked that they were listening to my ideas, and I was getting to have a direct impact on how we were covering things," he said. "Just that freedom to take a crazy idea in my head and share it with people. It's great."

Also great for Burbank has been the access that the site has given him. That access and his lifelong love of Disney helped spur him on as he completed his first book. "The E-Ticket Life" was published in

2015 and chronicled how Disney has influenced his path so far, from his career to his love life; he met his wife at Walt Disney World and they honeymooned at Disneyland Tokyo.

That honeymoon trip actually helped pave the Burbanks' current park visitation trajectory. The Burbanks periodically visit the domestic parks but have spent more time of late in other nations (the real, passport-requiring variety, not the World Showcase variety), part of Burbank's effort to devote more focus on Disney's international properties. They're annual passholders at Disneyland Paris, and he said each country brings something unique to its own Disney experience. That might go against the persona created by the Disney Parks Blog, he said, but that sector of Laughing Place's business has grown as Instagram and other outlets have brought Americans across the pond on either coast and closer to the international experience.

"I like seeing how the Disney brand is interpreted in other parts of the world. France is a little different, but it also has devoted fans there. And if you go to a bookstore in Tokyo, you'll find all sorts of thick fan magazines. You can tell you are getting on a train there that's headed for Disney. Things are more buttoned up in the rest of the city. When they go to Disney, they feel the ability to let go and express themselves. They're wearing costumes, carrying popcorn buckets—it feels like it's been really internalized there," he said.

Burbank credits the work of his site and others that devote time to the international parks for kindling interest in those cross-border attractions. He's noticed that Americans are increasingly traveling overseas to visit those parks. In addition to the coverage from sites like Laughing Place, he feels that Instagram and redeemable credit card miles have helped push that trend. And, as he and his wife has discovered, visitors to those places are generally pleasantly surprised by the unique experience they have: "For nonfans, there's just an assumption that all of the theme parks around the world are the same. And, of course, that couldn't be further from the truth."

Perhaps even more so than the parks, Disney's various intellectual properties draw attention from around the globe. That creates problems for sites like Laughing Place, which have to determine how to devote resources that become more scarce with every acquisition.

"We've had a lot of editorial meetings about when to cover Fox stuff, for example, and to what degree. That's kind of necessitated needing more staff, but we don't want to be an FX site all of a sudden," he said. "We're trying to build out more of our 'Star Wars' and Marvel content. Maybe there are people interested in those brands who aren't necessarily interested in the rest of the company. We're trying to expand in ways that seem natural."

Those ways include channels devoted to Disney's ancillary properties and a "Star Wars"-themed podcast that launched not long ago. New staffers are brought in who, whether planned or accidental, are experts in these related properties and instantly add credibility to Laughing Place's coverage. But a balance needs to be reached between being comprehensive and offering coverage that's a natural fit for Laughing Place, he said. Not everything has worked, but Burbank said the Moseleys encourage a "fake it until you make it" approach and welcome creativity and experimentation.

That willingness to adapt with the times, and sometimes get ahead of them, has made the site a landing spot for many Disney fans. Laughing Place is in the enviable position of having to recruit a second generation of fans. Burbank said the site has probably faded from the memories of some former visitors, but their children are now discovering its content and making their own connections. That requires a whole lot of upkeep—visitors are just as likely to see new posts late on a random Friday night in late-May than during a Disney annual shareholder meeting—but it's a job for which Burbank and his team continually gain more passion.

"Our owners have been very dedicated to diving into things to learn everything there is to know. We're just going to write about things that generally interest us. It's been interesting to see how it all works out."

Sources:

1. https://web.archive.org/web/19990508220430/http://laughingplace.com
2. https://web.archive.org/web/19991011224347/http://www.irccomputing.com/DLTrivia/whoami.htm
3. https://web.archive.org/web/19990220043215/http://www.irccomputing.com/RodMiller/

CHAPTER EIGHT

Do Your Best Work, Then Try to Trump It

The Walt Disney Company was founded upon the notion that its content and products are meant for anybody and everybody. It did not matter the person's age, location, economic background, religion or race, they had a place in the Disney family.

In practice, though—at least in some respects—that may not be the case. One study done by Streetlight Data found that Walt Disney World's visitors were about:

- 80 percent white (the United States is roughly 76 percent white)
- 10 percent African-American (13 percent)
- 5 percent Asian (6 percent) [1, 2]

The Walt Disney Company does not report a demographic breakdown of its visitors. But anecdotal evidence seems to support these numbers and the notion that minority populations aren't as well-represented at the parks.

"I feel like it might be a financial thing," Victoria Wade, who focuses largely on Disney-related content at her Tea with V blog, said in a phone interview. "A lot of Black families may not be able to afford it ... the first time I went with my aunt when I was 8. My aunt took me with a youth group. So I didn't have those family experiences growing up."

Federal data shows that the average Black family earns nearly $30,000 per year less than the average white family. [3] Given that the average annual household income for a family visiting central Florida is about twice the average household income in Orlando—which, at $43,000, is even higher than the average Black household income of about $40,000—it could be a matter of some underrepresented populations simply being priced out of the fun. [4]

And that spills over into the content-creating community. There were members of the Disneysphere who were African-American and members of other minority populations, but most said over the years that they were isolated, grinding out a day's work like WALL-E seeking out their EVE while other parts of the Disney blogosphere were drifting around on the Axiom doing their thing in a more heterogeneous fashion. Erika Kurzawa, for one, said on her Castle Cravings site that a search for fellow Black content creators in 2017 yielded slim pickings: "We were lone creators, isolated within the same arena where we weren't yet certain we belonged." She was pleased to report that the community had grown a good deal by 2020, with more Black men and women meeting and building relationships forged by their passion for Disney. In Kurzawa's case, she was part of a group that liked to disneybound—emulate Disney fashion using whatever you had lying around or could scrounge up—and saw her group grow from five to 14 within a few years: "We were officially a community. And we'd finally found a home where we weren't just the token, Tiana or Iridessa in a group of our well-meaning white counterparts, but we ourselves had become a sisterhood. We had proven to ourselves and to each other that we belong in this space as much as anyone else." [5]

That's not to say that attempts to connect with the African-American and other populations online were lacking. The Walt Disney Company invited several Black female bloggers to an African-American Mom Bloggers mixer at Walt Disney World starting in 2008. Attendees, including Kimberly Coleman—who discussed the inaugural event on her Mom in the City blog—said the event was meant for Disney Parks to understand the bloggers' perspectives of the brand and get input on how to better connect with African-Americans in general. [6] The technology with which those women were making connections, including Blackberrys and web cameras (in HD!), may be laughable, but the experiences were anything but. Attendees reported being treated to a VIP experience and making connections with women—women like them—that they didn't know were out there in the Disneysphere.

"I had no idea there was so much to see, do, eat, touch, feel, enjoy and experience in not just an entertaining, but afro-positive, diverse, pro-Black, 'make you feel good about who you are' way. Quiet as it's kept, Disney is doing a great job of integrating the Black experience," LaShanda Henry, creator of Sista Sense and Black Moms Club, wrote about the 2009 trip—which occurred around the time that Tiana was introduced to the world in "The Princess and the Frog" and Barack Obama was inaugurated as the first Black U.S. president. "We often say every Black person needs to take a trip to Africa. After this weekend, I whole-heartedly feel like every Black person needs to be a part of the Disney experience because there is more for us there than I ever imagined." [7]

Only, some of those connections and positive vibes faded over time. Many of the participants from the 2008 and 2009 events have since gotten out of the content-creation game (the event as a whole seems to have faded away after a brief initial burst). And even those who took part didn't discuss solely Disney and/or theme parks, but rather sometimes mentioned Disney as part of their general lifestyle content. Thus, as the 2010s saw a surge in Disney-relate content from around the country and the world, minority populations were increasingly isolated.

"When I first broke into the community, it was very little from what I saw," said Wade, who started writing about the parks and the company after completing the Disney College Program, during which she worked in quick-service food at Hollywood Studios. "That's not to say there was nobody out there, but there was an oversaturation of white people."

Elantrice Hughley had similar observations. The Georgia native got hooked on Disney after a trip to Walt Disney World at age 5, along with a screening of *Herbie the Love Bug*. She said in an email interview that she launched her site, Diz Thru Brown Eyes, in 2011 after trying and failing to see many similar experiences from other African-Americans: "I wanted to join the blogging world due to not seeing anyone who looked like me express their love for Disney ... Black people do vacation at Disney Parks, sail on Disney cruise ships and are annual passholders."

Her site incorporates parks merchandise finds (including a Mean Muggin' Monday series), life observations as they relate to the parks and regular features on Black creatives who've been involved in Disney projects, including Jar Jar Binks actor Ahmed Best and *The Princess and the Frog* supervising animator Bruce W. Smith.

"With being a Black person, it was very important for me to share how Black people have been present with Disney," said Hughley, who works as a mental health professional for her full-time work.

Discussing the issue on her Theme Park Hipster Blog, Vaughn said the issue isn't necessarily at the top of her mind when she visits the parks, but after a while it could be hard not to notice: "When you get there as a Black person, you're so engulfed in the magic of Disney that you don't even pay attention to anyone else ... But then you start to notice, 'Oh snap, I'm the only Black person here.' But if you do see that Black family come by, you kind of give them that, 'Hey, what's up?' That nod. You don't even realize it until someone brings it to your attention. And then you realize, 'Wow, I'm really the only one here. Out of all these people. I'm passing by thousands of people, and maybe out of every thousand I see like a family.' But it is getting better. I do see a lot of people there. And maybe because of the age of social media where people's pictures on Instagram kind of inspire you." [8]

Vaughn tries to do her share of inspiring on her blog, podcast and Instagram feed. A central Florida native, she said she became enamored with theme parks long before her first Magic Kingdom visit in fourth grade, getting hooked by the likes of Sea World and smaller parks. By the time that first Disney trip came, she was already inspired to serve others in their theme park ventures, having grabbed every park map she could find so that she could be her family's guide to a park she'd never visited.

Walt Disney World was too expensive for her family to frequent, she said in a phone interview, but she fulfilled one childhood dream right after completing another one, buying an annual pass upon graduating with a doctorate of pharmacy degree. She remained in central Florida, moving to Tampa before settling in a house five minutes from the Magic Kingdom (close enough, she said, that she can see the nightly fireworks shows).

"I remember it making me so, so happy," she said of that annual pass. "But the day-to-day life of being an adult—I needed an escape to do something with the other talents. I figured, 'Why not do something where I can combine my loved of writing and making videos, and Disney?' "

That escape became Theme Park Hipster, which she launched in 2012. A couple Google searches and a natural inclination toward writing were all she needed to get started, but other aspects weren't as easy—how to drive traffic, for example. And then there was the fact she is a person of color trying to plant her flag in a world dominated (in many ways) by white men.

"When I started, I debated about putting my face online. That's something that a lot of people in this industry, white males, they don't have to think about," she said. "I didn't put my face on my site for two years. I didn't want people to go, 'Oh, she's Black. I don't want to read her blog.' "

And yet, she persisted. While acknowledging that it took a while for her to find her voice, Vaughn made a point to keep writing—and, a few years later, to start talking in the podcast she launched. Focusing as much on theme park history and travel advice (she's written a book on traveling to theme parks alone, "The Solo Theme Park Traveler's Guide"), she's built one of the larger libraries of content for any Black creator, and while she said representation in the Disneysphere has definitely grown it's still not where it should be.

"As far as the representation in the blogger world, it's pretty much you have to stumble upon someone," she said. "As far as someone who's really serious (about creating Disney content), I still don't see people. Disney does invite some lifestyle and mommy bloggers, but as far as people who take it more seriously, they're not invited. I talk about Disney all the time.

It's unfortunate, but it's not something I'm going to sit here and complain about. What's supposed to be given to the community, it will happen. It's still a work in progress. Being Black, you grow up this way so you are always used to having challenges. Things may happen a lot longer time away, they might happen slower, but they will happen."

As the Black Lives Matter movement continued to march more into the forefront of American society in 2020, Disney content creators rallied to support the African-American community. Among the blogs to run lists of Black Disney content creators were Melanie and Rochelle at Polka Dots and Pixie Dust, and Jada Welch at Popsugar. [9, 10] Jennifer Borget was among the social media users prominently touting the "Bibbidi Bobbidi Black" movement in 2020, devoting a month to celebrating all things Black (which, she pointed out, didn't have to be a "dirty word" or something that people should be wary of talking about).

"Not only is it important for Black children to see characters who look like them, but it's so impactful for other children (and adults, let's be real) to see diverse characters on TV, in books and other media," she wrote on Instagram. [11]

Wade said the movement started as a challenge of sorts, and she followed it in order to highlight fellow Black Disney content creators and learn more about minority representation in the company's history. But it was also meant to highlight what should be the company's role in boosting all portions of the population. The Walt Disney Company responded, touting its Supplier Diversity Team in 2020, which provided opportunities to business owners from all backgrounds. [12] Many Black creators say this push is neither too little nor too late, but it has been a long time coming both from the company and the creators who devote time discussing it.

"From the outside looking in, the marketing—you don't see it as much," Vaughn said of Black families being featured. "I don't know who they're trying to market. I don't know if we're being marketed to, but it can be better. There are Black families where this is their main trip. It is a big deal."

"In a perfect world, there would not have been a need for inclusion or 'push' because Black and white creators would be equal," Hughley said. "However, this world is not perfect, and neither is the Disney online community. Black Disney creators have always been creating content, being present in the Disney community but not getting the recognition deserved. Yes, there has been progress, but there is a long way to go for Black Disney creators to feel and be seen as equals."

Being seen equals starts at a young age for many people, according to Wade, who said there were very few African-American Disney characters for her to look up to in her youth. A teacher by trade, she sees in her students that having role models who look like them makes a difference in their self-esteem and perceptions of what their roles could be in society.

"With Disney being able to have that power to just create these characters and put them on display, they're a trillion-dollar company and they're doing this. It's really a big deal," she said. "I'm honestly so proud of how far we've come. We're not only creative, but we're supporting each other and working together. We can do the same thing as everyone else. I see more of it on my timeline now, and it's wonderful."

Sources:

1. https://www.streetlightdata.com/measuring-travel-behavior-disney-world/
2. https://www.census.gov/quickfacts/fact/table/US/PST045219
3. https://www.census.gov/content/dam/Census/library/visualizations/2018/demo/p60-263/figure1.pdf
4. https://pgavdestinations.com/news/attractions-industry-forecast-report-revealed/
5. https://castlecravings.com/blog/2020/disney-milaje-the-stylish-black-women-of-the-online-disney-community/
6. https://www.mominthecity.com/walt-disney-world-mom-blogger-mixer/
7. https://www.facebook.com/notes/black-business-women-online/2nd-walt-disney-world-african-american-mom-blogger-mixer/162832374666/
8. https://www.themeparkhipster.com/traveling-while-black-at-disney-world/
9. https://www.polkadotsandpixiedust.com/black-disney-creators/
10. https://www.popsugar.com/smart-living/black-disney-influencers-and-bloggers-47536758
11. https://www.instagram.com/p/B8aIDTHgLJT/
12. https://disneyparks.disney.go.com/blog/2020/02/leonard-spencer-when-everyone-participates-everyone-wins/

CHAPTER NINE

Having Fun Doing the Impossible

For most people who enter the Disneysphere, their final products have worked out only after a lot of trial and error. Most people who are born sound engineers, producers and general tech wizards don't devote their time to discussing why Maelstrom should never have been removed from Epcot or which Spaceship Earth narrator was the best. So those who want to spread the Gospel of Walt have to be self-educated on the best way to do so. And they often have to do so on relatively shoestring budgets, because there's no magic spell from a sea witch that will grant a neophyte podcaster an unlimited IT budget.

Some people, like Yaglenski, have some technological experience they can bring to the table to get things started. Others weren't so fortunate.

"The podcast was a thing I started pretty immediately, within a month. I went to Best Buy and bought a $20 microphone and Audacity software," Corless said of setting up the WDW News Today podcast. "It wasn't very good. Someone I met was nice enough to ask, 'Do you know how to get on iTunes?' I threw my hands up, 'I don't know, just please set it up for me.' "

Other origin stories have a similar sound.

"It was definitely a learning experience. I was basically at square one. I bought a $50 mic and downloaded

Audacity and basically just started recording," said Heaton, who had previously appeared on other podcasts relating to previous entertainment-related writing he did for movie and TV blogs. "I read a lot and saw YouTube videos about it. It's trial by error. I listen to them now and I think, 'Oh gosh.' "

He likely uttered some expressions a bit more blue than that early in his podcasting career, when he lost an entire Tomorrow Society episode due to sound issues. But the key for him was to just keep swimming and not let any hiccups deter him.

"Even if you read everything, whenever you're creating anything creative, it's almost like you have to create a bunch of episodes," he said. "For me, the tech side is a challenge. Whenever you think you've figured it out, they do another update on Skype and you have to learn it all over again. I still feel now like I'm OK, but I could be much better."

Wade's approach mirrors that somewhat. Tea with V represents a continual learning process, she said, with trial and error being one of her primary teachers. Vaughn learned via similar means, with the birth of her daughter showing her the importance of budgeting time—which is even more important than brushing up on the technical aspects of the hobby, she said. Juggling a family with a career and everything else that life throws at you made her realize that she can't take a week-to-week approach to Theme Park Hipster: "I have to plan my content out for a quarter. I'm recording five episodes in a day, then a few days later I maybe edit them, then get them scheduled. I do the same thing for blog posts—systems, processes and strategies. If I don't do it that way, stuff won't get done. I get up at 5 a.m. and start working on the blog. I have to do all that before everyone else wakes up."

While time is the major obstacle for some creators, others have had to adapt their technological offerings to maintain some sort of quality. The trio of Enchanted Tiki Talk only sprang for microphones after doing their show for a little while, relying upon Apple earphones with built-in mics and recording onto an iPhone or iPad early on. They've since graduated to recording on microphones utilizing Skype and say they're pretty comfortable now with the logistics of putting together a show from three different states.

Mongello said he's always been comfortable using technology and—like George Lucas in creating the "Star Wars" films—he had ambitions that outpaced the available technology at the time (he was, after all, working during a time when Disney fans had to download a ride score or background music loop from the likes of alt.binaries.multimedia.disney.parks rather than simply firing up YouTube). Knowing he had to leverage the audience he'd gathered with his book, Mongello was an early user of the former Ustream live streaming platform, using that to help push the envelope in terms of video content in 2007. He also experimented early on with 360-degree video, pushing himself to "be on the cutting edge of what's next," he said.

Being at the front of the technological rush has additional advantages. Yaglenski, for example, expanded his abilities to the point where he was hosting competing sites while simultaneously running InterCOT. And operations that reach a certain size need to factor in the internal tech they need to keep running. Corless for example, used to host a personal wiki page for various WDW News Today scripts. That became unwieldy over time, though, so he's converted to using Slack to share information among employees, with different departments utilizing their own channels. Staff meetings continue to take place via video chat, as well.

His staffers, like Mongello, tended to adapt quickly. Not everyone has the gift for gadgetry, though. DePaoli had a roommate who was willing to teach him the tech logistics of getting Dizney Coast to Coast going. The roommate told him that DePaoli would pick it up in a week. Four weeks later, he was finally comfortable enough with it to feel as though he could put out a decent product. He built up a more comfortable setting in time, and he's actually reached a point of maturity on the IT side of things where he now teaches a course on podcasting. But learning the tech is just one part of that, he stressed; gathering information and writing scripts and/or show outlines is another time-consuming part of the process. So is booking guests and/or outlining show topics, a process that often begins months ahead of time (with exceptions made for breaking news or rapidly changing situations like the coronavirus pandemic).

Hill said adequate preparation is easy to identify, both in determining when it's done and when it isn't.

"I'm not pulling stuff out of my butt. We've talked before, sometimes a week out. People don't want to sit there and listen to you read a script. But at least you've done the prep. You've done the research. I wish more people would do their homework before they get behind a mic. It pulls me out of the show when you (get something wrong when) you could have gone on Google and gotten the right date or even the right name."

The Tiki Talk trio had to learn some of that the hard way.

"The first few shows were pretty scripted. It's kind of hard to listen to now," Brown said. "Now, we choose a topic and talk about it, but it just gets extremely sidetracked and we'll just start to talk about stuff and throwing around sayings and movie quotes. Because we know each other so well, it's not a show. It's just us talking as friends with a beer in our hands. It comes off much better."

The final podcast product comes off much better, according to Heaton, when the creator learns solid producer skills. You don't want to overedit, he said, as elements like the occasional "um" or cracking of a soft drink can can only add to the realism and relatability of the discussion. But knowing where and how to shorten a conversation from time to time can make the final product subtly—but noticeably—better. He also credits the guest for "90 percent" of the final production value.

Adding personal flourishes, of the technological kind or otherwise, can also make one stand out. Heaton had his brother-in-law write the theme music to his show. Dizney Coast to Coast opens every episode with an all-time earworm of a kazoo jingle, while anyone who's listened to WDW Radio knows they can strap in once Mongello tells them to "sit back, relax" and enjoy that episode's offerings.

Bloggers have also had to evolve. Frost has had to update the look and feel of Disney Blog, along with its content management system—which can much more easily accommodate photos and videos than CMS platforms in his early days. But he maintains the same production schedule he always has writing his stories in a word processing document and then cutting and pasting them into the CMS.

"There's a lot more support now in terms of plug-ins. You can do a lot more crazy things with your blog. Whatever you were writing earlier on, you were limited in your image size and quality," he said. "Now there are more web resources."

Those tools include analytics, which Frost said have helped him fine-tune his offerings as he's mastered how to best use them to his advantage. For example, he's learned that Google frowns upon excessive linking—which has caused several syndication-only operations to close up shop over the years—so he's adapted to attempt to do more original reporting. Reading the data has showed him that Disney Blog fares best when it's among the first sites to deliver a piece of breaking news, and when it offers updates on new additions or changes coming to the parks. Maximizing the analytics has helped him reach between 5,000 and 10,000 people per day, and sticking to what delivers the best results helps drive home consistency with his readers.

"People who can't get there all the time count on us to provide them with what's new and what's coming next in the parks," said Frost, who noted that some subgenres like Disney baby-related items and merchandise photos also drive good numbers.

Frost noted that one of the biggest technological aides remains one of the first that was available. Among the few regrets he has about the Disney Blog is that he never started an email list, which is one of the strongest sources of traffic for bigger sites (email open rates for entertainment-related entities average nearly 15 percent). [1] Now, most content creators offer some sort of newsletter or other subscription sign-up on their page, as that remains a better traffic source than any social media outlet (entertainment-related social media click-through rates hover around 0.5 percent). [2]

The first step for content creators, it would then appear, would be to understand what this terminology means. The second would be to adapt to some degree, even if they're not completely willing to toss away all of their old ways of doing things. Hill, for one, has come a long way from his days of churning out copy from a typewriter, but from his point of view all of the latest advances are mere tools and don't mean much unless they're properly used.

"These things make it easier, but at the same time you still have to be a storyteller. Identify, 'That's interesting. That's not.' Have respect for the audience and their time," he said.

That respect extends to respecting audience expectations. "Come hell or high water," he said he and co-host Len Testa are committed to recording another episode of their The Disney Dish podcast to be released every Monday; a schedule of five other podcast is also religiously abided by. Mongello also remains rigidly on schedule because he knows his audience does the same: "We're creatures of habit. Unlike a blog or even a video series, it becomes your routine. People have an expectation that you set every week to have (a podcast) at a certain date or at a certain time."

DePaoli shares that sentiment, with nary a gap in his twice-weekly recording schedule (other than an annual holiday break).

"I am a very 'consistency is key' person. I really take the promise to the audience super-seriously," he said. "If I only did it when I was really in the mood, it would not be two a week."

Same goes for Hill. Via an assist from his ex-wife and an old friend, Jim Hill Media was established soon after he parted ways with Laughing Place in 2003 ("I was in my obnoxious phase," Hill said of his time working with the Moseleys, "they were more of a play-nice group."). He ran his Disney coverage through that site through the next decade-plus, reveling in the fact that "finally there was a site that couldn't fire me" (in addition to Mouse Planet and Laughing Place, Hill worked for a site called DCA Central for three years that abruptly closed in 2004, and a four-stint with Huffington Post ended in 2018 when he was told he no longer was suited to reach that site's target demographic). During that time, he went to a Mega Mouse Meet gathering of Disney content creators through the invitation of Deb Wills. The group was posing for a photo when fate struck.

"I went to the back of the photo and stood next to some skinny guy, and he makes this obnoxious comment that gets me to chuckle. That's how I met Len Testa."

Testa had already authored "The Unofficial Guide" series for years at that point for the various parks and Disney Cruise Line. He'd also established his Touring Plans project as part of a graduate school thesis, using the tech that some other content creators had been wary of to improve Disney fans' lives. While waiting in line for the Great Movie Ride—out in the Florida sun, before the ride queue wound inside the structure to any great degree—he was inspired to write a computer program that could help guests do the parks more efficiently and avoid lines. Three years' worth of data collection allowed him to make park optimization part of Unofficial Guide series. [3]

But Hill didn't know that at the time, striking up a friendship that ended up berthing the Disney Dish podcast in July 2011. It was by no means planned, Hill said, but it's become the cornerstone of a network of podcasts Jim Hill Media operates.

"Both Len and I share a sense of humor and we share a sensibility. It's Disney and it's very enjoyable ... but at the same time it's a business. If you can push past all the wishes and the dreams and the magic, there's a lot of fascinating stuffing going on. I'm the old fart. I'm the guy who knows the history. He has the facts, I have the history," he said.

That background has served Hill well and reinforced what he's doing during moments when the technology might otherwise slow him down. He said the key for any content creator is to keep the foot on the gas, whether it's upgrading their tech skills or in any other facet of the operation.

"You totally have to be a self-starter. You have to deliver your own stuff without somebody cracking the whip," said Hill, who noted the struggles are different yet equally real for current event sites and nostalgia operations like some of his efforts. "I work the history beat. I have been doing this since 1984. I don't have to go to a park to dig up a story. I can just pull back into the files and pull something up and spit it out. It's the tool set that I developed in print that made it easier to adapt."

Disney Dish podcast is accompanied by shows about animation, Marvel and LucasFilm, among others. The network has sustained itself only because of the consistency Hill, Testa and his other collaborators bring to the operation, in his opinion.

He's picked up the technical and other aspects of podcasting along the way. A big lesson for him was to avoid long-windedness.

"If we do an hour-long show, we're thinking that's a little long. People have things to do. People get their slab of entertainment and news. So many people who do these things are self-indulgent. I don't have three hours of interesting stories to tell," he said, reiterating that fine-tuning such aspects of his business are the result of a lot of hard work. "You can't make the mistake of repeating yourself. It's a challenge for all of us to stay relevant. In a lot of ways, I'm a lucky guy. The harder I worked, the luckier I got."

Whether delivering three hours' worth of content or three minutes, creators widely agree that they key is to bring a touch of professionalism to the job—that way, even if there are technological or other shortcomings, they can be made up for (and the credibility of the site saved) by the creator's sound principles.

"I have a communications degree. I was involved in a lot of college journalism. I brought those journalistic principles with me to writing online," Frost said. "I don't have a fact-checker. I don't have a copy editor. I am those things, but I tend not to publish rumors unless I have a second source or without explanation of credibility. Being authentic and transparent are key principles for any blogger, and I try to keep those central when I'm thinking about things."

Mongello feels there's some room for flexibility within this structure. He encourages listeners and readers to offer ideas for what they'd like to see featured on his content network.

"Make sure they have a vested interest," he said. "There's so many different ways to approach it. Try to do a shot that's interesting and valuable to everyone from the casual Disney visitor to the hardcore fan who would appreciate a deep dive."

Sources:

1. https://www.smartinsights.com/email-marketing/email-communications-strategy/statistics-sources-for-email-marketing/
2. https://strikesocial.com/blog/click-through-rate/
3. https://www.coaster101.com/2018/08/07/len-testa-and-touringplans-com-part-one-the-origins/

CHAPTER TEN

Tough Competition: Wouldn't Know How to Get Along Without It

The online Disneysphere has certainly come a long way since the Clinton administration. A lot of the major players gained their status simply by joining the Mickey Mouse club early on and weathering the years. A few lucky entrants who were relatively late to the party were comprehensive or unique enough to carve their own niches in the marketplace. But finding new angles to discuss has become a near-impossible task as the 21st century progresses.

"It's so hard to grow an audience," Duffy said. "We don't really try to grow anything anymore. Blogging is even harder to make a name for yourself. People stick to the main ones."

That doesn't stop people from trying (as it shouldn't). If there's a subset of Disney culture out there, chances are that someone's online discussing it.

- Do you know a person with a handicap who's thinking about making a trip? Send them over to Disabled Disney.
- Want to maximize your bang for the buck? Check out Mouse Hacking, which details discounts, mile redemption opportunities and other money-saving strategies (this sector of

the blogosphere has perhaps the most entrants, some of whom are travel planners or other professionals who run the sites to complement their business operations).

- Looking to freshen up your lanyard? You need to visit the Disney Pins Blog.
- Want to visit with a serviceman or woman? Don't go before you browse through Military Disney Tips Blog.
- Are you a young professional who's looking for some Disney fun before settling down? The Childless Millennial Pretzel Co. is made for you.
- Looking to take a deep dive into Disney lore? Visit Disney Nerds.
- Want some advice on navigating the parks with a child? To Infinity and a Blog might just have the answers you seek.
- Do you maintain that your first visit to Walt Disney World as a kid was the best one? Retro WDW might spark some nostalgia with podcasts discussing lost attractions and restored ride and promo videos.
- Did that Disney Vacation Club saleswoman in front of Toy Story Land captivate your family into considering taking the financial plunge? The DVC Duo might push you over the edge.
- In love with a particular resort? The Wilderness Princess has pretty much every secret that exists about Wilderness Lodge.
- Raised by the Mouse was created to cater to plus-sized park-goers who might feel excluded from some attractions at times but deserve to feel the same magic as everyone else.

Just how many blogs, podcasts, vlogs and other Disney content sites are there? There's no real way to devise an answer to that without scrolling through a Google search until you're Carl Fredricksen's age. But there are enough to allow someone researching the subject to scroll through multiple top 100 lists and not only see no duplicates among the lists but not come across a single Disneysphere member whose content they actually consume.

"Especially now in what is a very noisy ... I don't think of it as a competition, but it is a very crowded space, and it is a competition for some," Mongello said.

The options are overwhelming enough to induce crippling anxiety, honestly—and that's both for the realm of topics that are covered and for the amount of content creators who devote their work to a given site (Googling "Disney vacation blog," as one example, yields 57.5 million results—and amazingly enough, the Disney-operated site isn't the top result). There's a choice to satiate the cravings of every type of Disney or theme park fan, but to get started in the Disneysphere is a bit like trying to merge into a Piston Cup race at the halfway point, everyone going at full speed and so engaged in what they're doing that you almost can't help but get passed by and quite possibly run over.

In other words: ka-chow.

"People don't realize it's very hard to attract an audience," said Duffy, who's been part of a team that's managed to maintain enough of an audience to top 300 Enchanted Tiki Talk episodes.

Getting found is among the biggest challenges for anyone starting out. There were more than 1 million podcasts in existence as of April 2020. Half of all U.S. homes had at least one person in them who calls him or herself a podcast fan, with 24 percent of the population listening to at least one show weekly. [1] So, while there are a lot of potential listeners, there are more shows than there are animatronic happy singers in It's a Small World.

That, according to Frost, is right up Disney's alley.

"They reach out to a diverse base of bloggers and podcasters, and they can now target toward specific interests. There's a menu that they're trying to fill, a product mix," he said.

If the number of podcast options seems like a lot, consider there are 152 times as many blogs to choose from, with two new blog posts every second. About 77 percent of internet users say they regularly read blogs, which is part of the reason that one-fourth of all the websites in existence are blogs. But more than 70 percent of readers say they'd prefer video if given the option, forcing most content creators to increasingly pivot in that direction in order to have any shot of breaking through. [2] The numbers indicate that's the way money is flowing; the number of six-figure YouTube channels is growing by 40 percent a year, with 1 billion of hours devoted to watching YouTube content worldwide each day. [3] YouTube has generated a series of millionaires, with the top earner of 2019, Ryan Kaji, bringing $26 million—more than $3 million for each of the eight years he's been on Earth. [4] One top YouTuber, Irishman Sean William McLoughlin (who posts under the name Jacksepticeye), was actually recruited by Disney to create be part of the series "Polaris: Player Select" on Disney XD and host a D23 gaming panel. [5,6]

So there's a lot to be gained by devoting time to becoming an Internet sensation—if that's your goal and if you have the time for it. Most kids and young adult gamers would have that time, but for adults creating Disneysphere content who have lives offline, simply knowing they brightened the lives of a few consumers would be enough—although that's a Herculean task in itself, even for those who have been around the block a few times.

"Sometimes you just looked away. You didn't want to admit what was coming," said Yaglenski, who noted that those who are successful on the internet, whether in the Disneysphere or otherwise, tend to stand out for who they are as much as what they create. "You could kind of see it. There was an element of denial. In retrospect, I should have made myself more of a personality than I did. Had we jumped all over doing vlogs earlier on, we probably wouldn't have lost as much audience as we lost."

InterCOT had an audience to lose, although it's still considered by the Walt Disney Company to be big enough to be an influencer. WDW News Today has grown audience year after year through a comprehensive approach, churning out assembly line-style content across all content areas. Readers will notice, Corless said, and learn to come to you first given enough time: "They know whatever's going on that day, someone from our site is there. Whatever it is, they know we have it."

Many sites would love to eventually build up to that point, but their creators have to find a balance between feeding their passion and feeding their families. It's easy to whistle while you work on your pastime, after all, but when it actually becomes work the apple tends to get poisoned.

"It's a real challenge to find time," said Heaton, who said he fits in 20- or 30-minute intervals to work on the Tomorrow Society at night, on lunch breaks and other times when he's not caring for his wife and two girls. "I'm looking at it in terms of I'm going to do this for me and it's important, but I'm not going to take away from anything else I'm doing. When you do the actual work, a lot of it is just carving out 20 minutes,

30 minutes. I'm never in a position where I'm going to do a blog post every day."

That means that content creators like Heaton have to focus on quality rather than quantity if they're going to break through. Where sites like WDW News Today and WDW Radio have the volume of content to be heard in the internet abyss, most others have to get creative in their topics. WEDWay Radio falls back upon the "endless topics" relating to the history of the "multifaceted conglomerate" that Disney has become, Parrish said. History-based creations like his have the advantage of tapping into a vast resource that has roots going way back.

"Walt was nostalgic," said Parrish, who noted that ideas of futurism were a big part of life for Walt and countless other people dating back to World War II. "Then in the 2000s, nostalgia became more important again. People sort of celebrated the past in ways people hadn't before. When you get in a post-Sept. 11 era and you see little things are a little more volatile, you look back and see things as more comfortable or easy. The ideas and the concepts about how science was an end, that's not the way that people see science today, unfortunately."

Other creators tap into what they do well. Enchanted Tiki Talk's trio likes to let the humor and improvised banter of Brown, Holley and Duffy shine through. And Heaton said paying attention to details can help a show like Tomorrow Society stick out.

"In general, podcasts are increasing across the board," he said. "If you're a big Disney fan, you're not going to listen to 100 podcasts. The biggest thing is just having a point of view. It doesn't mean you can't be like other shows. There are tons of shows about news, a lot of history shows. The best ones have a certain level of production competence, but that only goes so far."

That thirst for consumers might drive some content creators too far in the direction of stirring controversy for the sake of some eyeballs and clicks, according to Hill. He's all for regular reports on park updates, but they can get a tad annoying when someone's reaching to stir the pot.

"I saw a story once about a bench falling apart. In order to get a strong photo, someone pulled it apart to make it worse," Hill said. "You are surrounded by 50 attractions. A parade's about to go by, and you're going to fixate on the fact that some slats on a bench are broken. They really sometimes can't see the forest from the trees. People will save for years to take their families down for this once-in-a-lifetime vacation. They lose that perspective. That's a mistake."

Having more entrants into the Disneysphere has caused the competitive juices to boil over a bit. News sites like Laughing Place have to try and beat other sites to the punch and get content out before it's old news, but since Disney got into the game it's more often now a race to see which sites can be first to syndicate it or quote-source that information.

"We keep on top of what other people are posting to some degree," Burbank said. "There is a saturation point on certain aspects of it. The Disney Parks Blog made things easier and harder at the same time. It's an outlet for official news that's reliable, but no one will have that big of a scoop anymore because Disney will beat you to it. There's more room to be original when you bring in perspective. We might cover some of the same stuff, but we cover more of the movies and everything about the business side and earnings calls—we live blog those."

Heaton found a niche of sorts in a running trip report he recorded during a 30-hour solo trip to Walt Disney World in summer 2019 to get first impressions of Star

Wars: Galaxy's Edge. During that trip, he chronicled every up and down, from the value resort experience to the intolerably long bus lines and, yes, blue milk. Despite running largely on fumes at points, he got that show and gets the rest of his content out in a timely manner. Such mannerisms help listeners and readers find a content creator they can trust, in his opinion.

"It's a daily challenge for anyone to discover you. That's just something, because you have to and you try to do your best. Have to be consistent," he said. "Not, 'You have to have hot takes.' You have to have some perspective. My perspective is I went to Walt Disney World when I was a kid. Went once a year. My point of view is what interests me. I just want to talk to smart people about theme parks. You could have greatest idea ever, and it's hard for people to find you. A lot of it is timing. ... There's no secret sauce. It's a daily challenge. At some point you just have to be happy with, 'If I was standing in a room and talking to that many people, it would be amazing.' "

The competition can extend to interview subjects, as well. Anyone who's made their way through the Disney podcast circuit will recognize certain names that pop up again and again. It works, of course, because each show brings its own spin to the interview. But there has to be some balance between an interesting story and name to advertise on the virtual marquee.

"I'm not looking to find people who are more obscure. I'd love to talk to the biggest names available," said Heaton, who said consuming other content and scouring social media can help a creator find interesting subjects. "I try to build credibility by mentioning friends of the guests that I might know. Sometimes my shows, I'll reach out to someone and we'll record a show eight months later. You can't think it's going to be next week and plan that way. You have to build that rapport up front ... When you're trying to get guests, it's always a challenge. You have to cast a wide net, be persistent and then take a chance."

Some of those interviews could be granted to online creators at the expense of mainstream media outlets, which have had to adapt to the challenge. Hill recalls the first time the Disney Parks Moms Panel was invited to a press event that he was at. With the Wall Street Journal and New York Times situated six rows back, the Disney moms were ushered in and allowed to take up the front rows.

"Those are the social media influencers for the company ... to watch these legacy media guys get their noses bent out of joint was something," he said. "First of all, get over yourself. The world isn't going to end if you don't write your story about the tilt-a-whirl. Who makes the decisions in the household about the vacation? The mom. More power to them. You've got to adapt. Learn to roll with the punches."

Some content creators even make a living out of helping other people crack through the traditional-versus-digital divide. The Coffee Mom, who started blogging in 2016, has crafted a set of rules for how to get noticed and work with the Walt Disney Company as a content creator, among them creating a professional media kit to send to the company, requesting access and interacting with the company whenever possible—in other words, getting the company to notice you, if your end game falls into that realm at all. [7] Of course, producing something of at least competent quality is also important, but the company notices creators of all sizes, she said, so valuing their time will go a long way.

Mongello said he shares a similar approach. He said he built his audience organically, giving however many (or few) fans the owner's suite treatment, even if they paid for bleacher seats. That sort of respect and authenticity goes a long way, he said.

While everyone involved in the Disneysphere will acknowledge the crowded content field, there's also a funny synergy that exists within many members of that realm. Sure, they're ultimately competing for eyes and ears—and, ultimately, whatever dollars might be available—but creators generally don't want to see their success come at the expense of someone else. Rather, they want to see more people enter their briar patch, figuring there's always room for more. They're usually laudatory toward each other, willing and ready to encourage their fans to check out other sites, and quick with some words of encouragement for anyone trying to crack into the space (or, perhaps, write a book about said space).

That cooperative nature started early. Laughing Place ran a weekly feature in its nascent days highlighting some of the authors' favorite Disney-related sites. [8] InterCOT kept a running page of Disney-related sites that anyone was welcome to make recommendations or submissions for; Yaglenski also ran a sister site, Web Disney, that ran a directory of Disney sites through 2016, when it stopped being updated. [9] Sites like the Ultimate Disney Link Page and WebDisney existed solely to share Disney sites with the world, and groups like the Disney Webmaster Alliance helped everyone get a fairly level shot at access. [10, 11]

Even today, sites like Mouse Savers and Mickey Travels share links to some of their favorite sites. Touring Plans, meanwhile, sponsors the WDW Radio Newscast weekly live video show. And Laughing Place partnered with Dizney Coast to Coast to present the latter's weekly Sunday headlines show, which DePaoli said he'd previously gather and write himself. The House of Mouse Headlines show now features the best of Laughing Place's stories from the previous week with additional commentary. DePaoli, who has long had a good working relationship with Burbank, said the move was made in order to free up some time for him to focus on the regular Wednesday shows. It also strengthens his news offering, he said, and spreads the word about both sites to new audiences.

"Having worked with Jeff in the past, when the opportunity to grow that partnership and add in some small part to the production of the news episodes arose, it was really a no-brainer for me and the rest of the LP team," Burbank said upon the move's announcement in early 2020.

Wade said she frequently checks in with and speaks to other content creators, who generally are more than willing to lend an ear. There's a realization, she said, among many content creators that the competitive juices need not be flowing quite so freely: "The community is very, very large. We're all eating at the same table. So it's not like we're fighting for scraps. There's just a genuine kindness there."

Those sorts of kindness are common in the Disneysphere—if you know where to look and whom to seek it from—with friendships sparking from the most unusual spaces. It's often chance encounters—created through the products that are being produced on a weekly or monthly basis—that help some members of the community get to the next level.

"So much of where anybody ends up is the kindness of strangers. I would have never known writing Donald Duck would blow open the doors for me. There are great stories any time. It's a company full of story-tellers," Hill said. "There is some amazing citizen journalism going on. But at the same time, there's folks who approach it like, 'I may not have any facts, but I have an opinion.' A rising tide flats all boats."

Frost uttered the exact same quote during his phone interview, saying he and other reputable content creators have earned enough respect to maintain their following regardless of what else might be out there. He feels that there's plenty of landscape to cover so there's no reason not to be cordial and supportive—as long as new-media creators follow basic rules of decorum.

"Disney continues to invite bloggers and influencers and podcasters. I'm looking to give the audience information that they want. I don't particularly care who else is invited as long as they respect what I consider the rules: Don't steal content from others, don't step in front of (television and internet video camera) shots, behave nicely, realize that online media is not the most important media, most important is still print and broadcast, behave like invited guests. Because I have my following and I think they're pretty loyal to me, I go out of my way to help them. There's a lot more cooperation than there is competition."

Mentoring from the likes of Frost also helps usher in the next generation of Disney-lovers. Wade writes for DisKingdom in addition to her work with Tea with V and credits that site's owner, Roger Palmer, with getting her comfortable enough to branch out on her own: "He taught me about blogging and podcasting. A lot of my experience came from him. He was terrific."

Jimmy Horne from the Disney Nerds, which began broadcasting in 2013, has cited Yaglenski as a source of inspiration, saying InterCOT was his first Disney website. Yaglenski said connections like that go both ways: "Twenty years of friends. That's the whole thing. I've developed and cultivated a lot of relationships. Some are still there from day one."

Vaughn, meanwhile, got some help after reaching out to Mongello—who takes pride in boosting the efforts of others and also was quick to deliver that "rising tide" quote. The two began working together in early 2020 after years of Vaughn tuning in to WDW Radio and several other shows: "They were the keys to how I got started. To have him help me be a better content creator, a better community builder—it's kind of like working with Michael Jordan."

Not everyone can be like Mike, but there's plenty of room on the basketball court for everyone, and the majority of content creators will unite behind each other. DePaoli said he's seen this collaborative nature several times. Among them was in 2017, when the Los Angeles Times was banned from an early screening of "Thor: Ragnarok" due to the paper's investigation into the Walt Disney Company's business dealings with the Disneyland host city of Anaheim. The company cited a "disregard for basic journalistic standards" in making the move. But mainstream and online journalists and content creators—as well as movie directors like Ava DuVernay—united in boycotting the company's offerings or otherwise calling the company out, resulting in a swift reversal. [12]

"When this happened, it only got reversed because other publishers said, 'This isn't how you treat journalists. This person was just doing their job,'" DePaoli said. "It's good to have that unity. There's a lot of it."

Even when covering the same event, digital content creators have been able to get along with their traditional counterparts—and each other. Frost said at most events he attends with limited guest/celebrity availability, content creators have managed to share the space in an amicable fashion and ensure that everybody got their questions asked and quotes jotted down. That wasn't necessarily always the case early on, he said, but the overriding sense of cooperation has crept in more as time has passes.

Of course, as in the case of that L.A. Times journalist, the Walt Disney Company ultimately decides who (at least at a press level) gets access to the company and its latest happenings. That could force any feelings of synergy, at least at certain times and for certain events, to be left at the security check. Many creators pride themselves on either earning press credentials—meaning they maintain a neutral stance—or pay their own way to the parks, meaning they can't be beholden to the company in exchange for access. It's only human nature not to feel some sort of gratitude, according to DePaoli, if the company grants you access—"anyone with a soul would feel that way," he said. But creators who need access in order to gain extra clicks or views might be tempted to cross over the line from editorial into advertorial.

"We try and do a positive, fun show, but if one is being real, if there's something we don't like, we have to say it. We don't drink the Kool-Aid as some do, but it is hard to distinguish yourself between shows," said Brown, who like most other people who were interviewed wasn't interested in calling anyone out by name.

The temptation is easy to understand, especially when you're talking about food at the parks (quick-service meals including drinks generally run around $20 per person, according to an analysis of the official Disney parks menus, while sit-down meals can easily top $60 per person). But A.J. Wolfe, for one, resists any possible urge not to splurge. Founder of the Disney Food Blog, her job (as much of a struggle as it is) is to wolf down multiple meals per day when she visits the parks (she lives in Texas and makes regular visits but has staff near both U.S. parks). She told People that, even though some comps probably could be had, she prefers to foot her own bill: "I've had managers try to pay for my food, and I'll go up to them and say, 'I'm sorry, but this is something that we have to pay for in order to remain unbiased for our readers.' And, frankly, it's better for them as well because if I have to write a review that says you paid for it and it's a good review, nobody's going to trust that." [13]

Hill said he's been able to work with some divisions within the Walt Disney Company, but a reluctance to completely toe the company line has created occasional grief for him and Testa—and he wouldn't have it any other way: "They often want stories told in a certain way, and that's not how Len and I work. We'll tell the truth. We'll step beyond the wishes and the dreams and the magic."

DePaoli, who said he's occasionally heard from individuals who have worked on things in Disney but never the company itself, feels authenticity like that carries through to the listener: "If Disney has an issue with me, it is worrisome sometimes, but I honestly think that podcasts like mine are full of honest opinions and not just praise are the best kind of marketing. I'm going to let you know the problems, and I'm going to praise the things that are amazing. They're only going to paint themselves in a good light, so you can't really trust that. The latest churro is not the greatest thing to come to the Disney parks in the last 20 years."

Most creators agree that if your motivation is to curry favor with the Mouse House and get the occasional free ticket or piece of swag, you won't last very long—not because that intent leads to failure in and of itself, but it's not a long-term driver. Once that goal is achieved, you'll have nothing else to strive for, so the desire to keep going will quickly wane. Rather, only those with an incessantly burning flame of passion for something related to Disney and the parks will achieve true long-term success—even if that success can't be measured in dollars.

"We have people who we tweet with and talk to who have recognized us in parks, on cruise ships. We did a meet-and-greet at the parks and people actually showed up," Brown said of him and his Enchanted Tiki Talk partners. "It's amazing to see three or four guys who enjoy something that connects with thousands of people. It's inspiring, really. We all have our down days, and then we take and read a tweet or an iTunes review. It's inspiring to know that we can bring that joy into a person's week in a small manner."

And regardless of who's delivering that joy, Mongello said the important part is that the joy is received. To this day, he counts among his greatest pleasures hearing from a listener or viewer that one of his shows brought joy to that person's day. The parks are a main source of that sort of joy for countless people who have been lucky enough to visit them, he said, so rekindling that feeling really is the best reward—and it's OK if the spark comes from somewhere else.

"The numbers have grown, and that's a good thing. The medium has become so much more accessible. The gatekeepers are gone. You used to have to find a publisher, someone to put you on radio or TV. There's room for us all. We can all win. It's not like terrestrial radio or watching TV where you have to choose at 5 what you want to watch.

"I think it makes everybody better, too. Having other things that can be fighting for your attention forces everybody to be better, and I love that. We as consumers, we benefit as a result."

"If we're going to succeed, we're going to succeed together," Wade said. "We all have the same goals, and it's to bring our readers quality information."

Sources:

1. https://www.podcastinsights.com/podcast-statistics/
2. https://99firms.com/blog/blogging-statistics/#gref
3. https://www.omnicoreagency.com/youtube-statistics/
4. https://www.forbes.com/sites/maddieberg/2019/12/18/the-highest-paid-youtube-stars-of-2019-the-kids-are-killing-it/#127efbfc38cd
5. https://twitter.com/disneyd23/status/883350234503421953?lang=en
6. https://www.tubefilter.com/2017/06/15/disney-xd-maker-studios-jacksepticeye-parkergames-strawburry17-tv/
7. https://www.thecoffeemom.net/2019/11/29/how-to-work-with-disney-world-as-an-influencer/a
8. https://web.archive.org/web/19990909235908/http://www.laughingplace.com/default.asp?WCI=SitePick
9. http://www.intercot.com/disneynet/default.asp
10. http://www.tudlp.org/
11. http://www.webdisney.com/
12. https://www.nytimes.com/2017/11/07/business/disney-la-times.html
13. https://people.com/food/disney-food-blog-aj-wolfe-walt-disney-world-restaurants/

CHAPTER ELEVEN

Music You Can Taste, Color You Can Smell

Let's pretend these are the first words you're reading of this book, and you have no idea what it's about.

Walt Disney World.

Quick, what's the first thing that came to your mind?

Mickey-shaped pretzel? Dole Whip? I know, Starbucks in the Magic Kingdom?

For many people, food is one of the main, if not the primary, source of pleasant memories when traveling, whether to the Disney Parks or anywhere else (try separating Islands of Adventure from Butterbeer, or wings from Buffalo). Not everyone likes rides, fireworks or stage shows.

But everyone eats.

Which makes food the dominant niche that exists in the Disneysphere. But it's hardly the only one, and most of them have been filled. The lucky few who got there first—or did that subset best—have earned the right to rule that section of the internet. Some niches were filled early on in the internet's life span. Frost recalls seeing early sites devoted to specialized areas such as the flowers of Walt Disney World, the landscape of Disneyland and interview sites featuring discussions with cast members who remained part of the Walt Disney World since its 1971 opening day (at that time, it would have been around a two-decade span).

Those with the right combination of inspiration and perspiration can develop a new area to devote their time to. Vaughn, for one, realized there was a significant enough subset of solo Disney travelers out there to warrant her devoting time to that subject on Theme Park Hipster. Some people still balk at the mention of going to Walt Disney World by themselves, but she insists it's the sort of experience every Disney fan should strive to have at least once.

"It's a very freeing experience. The first time it is scary and it is nerve-wracking, especially if you're coming from another state. And you're used to navigating the airport with other people," she said. "There's something about that freedom when you get there. Like if you have plans, but something else catches your attention. When you're with a group of people, they might be like, 'What are you talking about? We have Tower of Terror passes.' And you tend to meet other solo travelers. You see them and you're like, 'OK, you're crazy like me.' You have the freedom to decide. Doing that at a place like Walt Disney World: 'All of this is my place? This world is my oyster? OK, now what do I do?' "

Many other niches have been filled over the years. Touring Plans utilized data and science to make it a go-to source for predicting park crowds and other visitor-related details (although Shannon Albert at WDW Prep School puts her own solid spin on the subject matter). Sarah Stone and Don Munsil have taken over Waring's work at Mouse Savers and made that among the pre-eminent sites for destination information (with Testa acting as one of the site's contributors). Melissa, David and Gillian Temple have mastered helping people of all ability levels work their way through the parks on Disabled Disney. The Disney Cruise Line Blog and Disney Pins Blog … well, you know.

And while the words "churro" or "giant turkey leg" probably just generated a Pavlovian response as you read them, few sites devoted much attention to Disney parks food—at least as a standalone element—until Wolfe came along in 2009 (Corless did take an early stab at it with dining.wdwnewstoday.com, but the idea of a standalone site didn't take off in 2007). The fact that the name Disney Food Blog was even still available in 2009 serves a testament to the relative obscurity that segment of the Disneysphere wallowed in through the first 15 years or so of mainstream internet use.

The native of Jamestown, N.Y.—just south of the hometown of this book's author, Buffalo—offered a simple answer in an email interview when asked what sparked her to create her enterprise: "It didn't exist, and I wanted to read a website like it." She would scour the internet for whatever Disney-related food content she could find, including message board threads, but the experience always left her craving more. Now living in Dallas, Wolfe said she spent more time planning her meals than anything else when she made a trip to the parks—something that My Disney Experience app has now almost made a requirement for Walt Disney World visitors—and she figured if she couldn't find a resource on the subject, she'd provide that service for others.

She'd connected with food at the parks early on. Her parents would make the drive from Western New York to Florida every few years, she told Zannaland, and among her early memories was stopping at a kiosk at Epcot to make dining reservations and being introduced to new (and sometimes less-than-appetizing) options. But one random snack has left quite the aftertaste: "One food memory that will always stick with me is of a little clear plastic box filled with tiny tarts candy. Disney sold them at MouseGears in Epcot, and you could get other types of candy besides tiny tarts, but I coveted that little box with the Disney World logo on it and all of the rainbow-colored candies inside." [1]

So Wolfe set out to create the sort of website that would be her favorite place to visit if she hadn't created it, the kind to rekindle those sorts of memories for everyone who visited. The site's first post, aside from a basic introduction, was about Dole Whip and introduced a Snack Series that's proven popular for the Disney Food Blog. Other subsets the site introduced include a eating healthy section, birthday treats that can be had at Disney restaurants, first-timer must-tries and a "The Best Thing I Ever Ate in Disney" series featuring readers' favorites. And every post (as well as the enterprise's social media feeds) is photo-heavy, because if one is being honest no amount of words (nope, not even 1,000) can make up for one mouth-watering photo. So the site had the food scene covered. But Wolfe wasn't sure how hungry the Disneysphere was for her content initially.

"There was almost a stigma attached to talking about food because people thought it was weird to care so much about Disney restaurants," she told People. "I remember thinking, 'Will people read this? Is that going to be weird? Who would ever go read a site about Disney food?' " [2]

As it turns out, a lot of people. The site quickly caught on, and the need was created to fill out and incorporate Disney Dining Plan details, restaurant menus and general food-related news. With demand growing, so did the supply of content. Wolfe said Disney Food Blog was the first site to purchase and try every single item at the Epcot Food and Wine Festival, and festival coverage has become a year-round mainstay for the site. Pretty soon, almost like trying the

Gray Stuff (Wolfe thinks it's delicious) or eating lunch next to Sonny Eclipse, checking out the Disney Food Blog became a must-do part of the process of visiting the parks. Given the cost of eating at a Disney property, it makes sense for visitors to want to know what they're getting into and try to maximize their spending power.

"Sometimes you spend more on your food than on your hotel or your park tickets," Wolfe said (and if you've ever eaten at Cinderella's Royal Table, you can confirm that and then some). "People celebrate with meals in Disney World. They look forward to the snacks they'll eat. It's a fun thing to think about and plan. Everyone has to eat, so it might as well be the best food possible."

Wolfe tries to keep tabs on the best food that's possible to obtain at the parks. Among her current favorites:

- The carrot cake cookie at Disney's Hollywood Studios
- The goat cheese ravioli at California Grill
- The wagyu beef at Morimoto Asia
- The Liberty Tree Tavern, she has written numerous times, is almost always the first restaurant she visits when she gets to Walt Disney World

But the site has information on everything from the best salty snacks at the parks to where to sit when eating at various quick-service restaurants and what the ingredient is in your favorite dish that you can't quite place. All of this information comes with some cost, of course. Wolfe runs the site as her full-time job from Texas. She has three regular contributors and numerous other hands on deck to cover everything going on both in central Florida and southern California. An array advertisers help fund the enterprise, as do sales of the Disney Food Blog Guide to

Walt Disney World Dining e-book and other digital guides the site sells.

Most people may not know what Wolfe looks like, but her voice and the shadowed white-font title cards to her YouTube videos have become a near-ubiquitous part of the Disney vlogging scene. The DFB Guide YouTube Channel racks in a good number of advertisements, thanks to the 550,000-plus subscriber base it's accumulated since its founding in 2016 (an older channel was upgraded to the current one at that time). Top videos on the channel—which, ironically enough, are on non-food topics such as "18 Things You Can Not Do in Walt Disney World" and "What I Wish I'd Known Before I Went to Disney World," have topped the 2 million-view threshold. Not bad for something Wolfe started almost more out of necessity than anything else.

"We wanted to be sure we had a footprint on that particular social space," she said. "But we had no idea it would become as popular as it has. We're grateful and honored."

Visuals, of course, are central to any food-related operation. She had some help on that front—her father was a photographer—but a lot of what she's learned about how take just the right picture was learned through practice, hours upon hours of practice. Among the techniques she cited on her site are:

- Experiment with camera angles, focus and camera settings so that you know right away what's the best option for a given situation
- Keep the surface clutter-free, as clean tables make for clean photos; the same goes for the plate itself
- Be ready with the camera immediately (the better to avoid temptation and eat first)
- Get a window seat during the daytime since

natural sunlight always makes for the best photos

- Shoot more photos than you'll need; you'll thank yourself later for giving yourself more options
- Don't forget the insides of the food, like the gooey gouda in a grilled cheese
- Practice at home so you can quickly get the job done and then get to eating

Wolfe feels her success with the site is as much about lucky timing as anything. Much like many other Disney-related sites that take off, the content that's offered happened to appear at a time when people started to notice that such content was lacking.

"We had a great idea whose time had come, so it hasn't been all that difficult to build up the audience. People were ready for a food-focused niche website about Disney," she said. "What is the most important thing is to keep creating great content that's valuable and useful to our readers, viewers and followers. If you create content that answers questions and provides value, you'll have an audience."

The audience for Disney food news and content has grown to the point where major TV and print media outlets in Orlando, Tampa, Los Angeles, Anaheim and neighboring cities now devote space to the subject, a shift in focus that Wolfe is partially to thank for. That means there are now a lot of spaces for people to fill up on food content, but Wolfe isn't concerned about the pack: "We don't really worry about it. If you create excellent content that is valuable to people. You'll have an audience. But I don't think people understand how difficult it is to consistently create excellent content. It's a lot of work."

Granted, it's work that most people would give their most cherished pair of Mickey Mouse ears to do, but it's still work. Which is why you should not be so quick to scoff at someone needing three minutes and seven takes to get just the right picture of their favorite quick-service meal at Pecos Bill Tall Tale Inn & Cafe. And not everyone is willing to take a bite out of such a substantial endeavor. But if you smile when you see that photo, fondly recalling the smells and tastes associated with it (and, let's be honest, we've all grinned like that at some point when checking out our feeds), that that work was well done.

Wolfe's food blog may be among the most well-known, but several others have helped satiate the cravings of consumers for Disney food content. A lot more feature food as part of a breadth of content options. Among other notable entrants primarily settles in the food subset:

- Allergy Free Mouse offers an assist to Disney-goers with allergen issues, giving tips on what dishes meet their needs and which should be avoided.
- Dining at Disney is where Kristen Hoetzel-Go and her staff write about and discuss parks-related food news and reviews, along with trip-planning tips.
- Food at Disneyland focuses on just that, with sections devoted to each park there as well as the Food and Wine Festival.
- The Healthy Mouse, where Jessica McDonald discusses more health-conscious recipes and other parks fare; she's also worked at expos at D23 and been part of the Disney Social Media Moms Celebration.
- Recipes of Disney is where Deanna Samaan plays with and replicates favorite parks dishes for home consumption; she also hosts a podcast there and a sister site, Seduction in the Kitchen.
- Vegan Disney Food is where Amanda Tinney

helps guests who want to eat well at the parks while avoiding animal-based products—a task she said can have some challenges but might not be as tough at one would initially think (Vegan Disney World also covers this realm).

- Straight from the source, the Disney Parks Blog features its own food and recipe sections, with submissions from parks chefs, concessions managers and other people who keep the magic cooking.

Sources:

1. https://zannaland.com/disney-food-blog-aj-wolfe/
2. https://people.com/food/disney-food-blog-aj-wolfe-walt-disney-world-restaurants/

CHAPTER ELEVEN

Who's Velocistar237?

Social media to a 21st-century content creator is pretty much like that tunnel Andy Dufresne had to crawl through to evacuate from the bowels of Shawshank Prison.

It stinks.

The contents have little to no value.

Being in it too much can literally makes you sick.

A lot of what you find in it is pure sh...

You get the idea. And then, when you finally work your way through it, there's not any light but rather a soaking rain. But it's the means to the end you need to achieve, so you endure it.

This may come as a shock to some of you readers, but a lot of people have strong opinions on the internet—especially if you, say, wear your face mask around your chin or hold a duck in the Magic Kingdom. And they are most certainly not shy about sharing them. Forums like InterCOT let people discuss the latest goings-on, however terrific or trivial, in a fairly civil manner. But then Mark Zuckerberg got drunk in his Harvard dorm room one night and launched what would become the social media revolution. Before long, anyone with a few spare minutes and the ability to hunt-and-peck a few sentences could put anything or anyone they wanted to on blast, oftentimes anonymously and without any sort of grammar, punctuation or spelling requirements.

First Facebook and MySpace let users share photos, songs and general thoughts about the parks and the newest developments at them, incorporating groups that could be joined so that participants could let their Disney flags fly freely. Then a few years later, Twitter put into place character limits and hashtags, giving users another way to (succinctly) opine about what should come to and go from the parks. It also introduced #DisTwitter to the lexicon, giving users a way to find fellow Disneyphiles or, depending on how it's used, deride portions of the online community that were considered to be outliers.

Corless' site was one of the first, along with Inside the Magic, to maintain a Twitter presence. He's since seen the highs and lows that come with social media and considers it to be a necessary evil, especially when a site is trying to build a brand—as long as you avoid the comment section.

"I listened to the social media noise early on. Those were the people who knew we existed," he said. "By the times things got truly toxic, we grew beyond (reading what was said about us). People are going to dislike the people they dislike. Now it's just so easy to piss on someone. If you succeed in this realm in any way, shape or form, you have to get used to the idea that you're going to be harassed."

Being first mattered, at least for a while. Frost was also among the early entrants into Twitter, joining in August 2007. That resulted in his site's Twitter remaining in the top five among Twitter Disney blog (no relation) searches for the first five years or so of the site's existence. His six-figure followership remains impressive by many standards—even Mongello trails him by nearly 100,000—but the algorithms give him no advantage for seniority, as far newer and less popular feeds tend to bump his and other, larger feeds down a few notches.

That's OK, though. It aids in the pursuit of discovering something new and perhaps stumbling into a new friendship. And a lot of good came of the connections that social media allowed. Among the thousands of Facebook groups relating in some way to Disney are groups devoted to:

- buying and selling Disney items
- dating fellow Disney fans
- visiting Walt Disney World as an adult
- the philosophies of Walt Disney
- annual passholders
- Disney park props, signs and posters
- pin trading
- Disney trading cards
- Disney Democrats

But as evolution has proven again and again, for every new advancement something else has to cede control.

"Social media killed discussion forums. The depth of discussions, the interaction you used to get was way more personal. It was way more cultivated," Yaglenski said. "You just don't get the same sense even today—and I wish we did—on Facebook and Twitter as you did on sites like ours. It feels a little more distant. I don't like the way things are nasty and where they go sometimes. The more connected we are, maybe this is just a side effect of that."

Frost isn't ready to tell internet discussion forums to bring their death certificates just yet, but he agrees that internet users in the times before social media tended to have manners that were more like Maui's and less like Constance Hatchaway's.

"That's the kind of spirit that I would like the whole online community to get back to," he said. "Just share cool content with each other. Before you know it, you've spent 10 hours learning about the Hatbox Ghost at the Haunted Mansion. That sort of old-school blogger spirit is what we need today to counteract the meaner or more sensational content."

Whether their intent is nice or nefarious, a lot of social media users—who conveniently can remain anonymous if they're not bold enough to put their faces to their words—can easily get caught down the rabbit hole that such sites can create. Some are genuinely curious about others' opinions. Others are itching for a good (virtual) fight. Still others are looking for the faux fame that shooting some straight fire can provide online.

"I'm constantly surprised, sometimes in a good way and sometimes disappointed, with social media especially. When you're protected by that veil of anonymity, it can be tough. But you have to ignore it—keep those blinders on," Mongello said.

"I think a trap that a lot of current Disney fans fall into is spending too much time in #DisTwitter world. People either think they need to have a hot take and be contrarian or agree with whatever the consensus is. People should not be afraid to say what they think. I think people just need to be more accepting. The Disney community is so big and diverse that of course not everyone is going to like everything," Burbank said.

That goes in particular for changes that come to the parks. The force remains strong among social media users who are still bitter a quarter-century after Horizons shut down, and the most aggrieved of them won't waste an opportunity to let everyone know. Fans of more modern attractions that Disney Parks are tinkering with (or even thinking about tinkering with) are quick to flood social media to let Disney know how dumb the move, and they in turn bring out the trolls who make fun of people who miss Maelstrom's trolls. Every Great Movie Ride fan's tweet seems to have an equal and opposite response. Neither side is wrong, per se, but many content creators say there's no need to wallow in such pungent toxicity.

"Maelstrom going away was, for some users, 'How do you do this?' For the mom and dad and the 7-year-old girl who hears *Frozen* is coming to Norway, Epcot—especially the World Showcase—becomes this incredibly attractive place that it wasn't before," said Mongello, who said he's embracing forthcoming additions such as the Tron coaster in the Magic Kingdom and the Spider-Man ride that's part of the Avengers Campus at California Adventure. "What's bad for one person is the best thing for somebody else. The place was never meant to be a museum ... People lost their minds on Twitter about the Tower of Terror leaving California Adventure. And a lot of them love the Guardians of the Galaxy in there now. I have faith in Disney that they know what they're doing. While it might not initially make sense, 99 percent of the time it seems to end up making sense in the end."

Burbank brings a similar approach to Laughing Place: "I'm one of the few Disney fans where I don't have a ton of sacred cows in the park. It's sad to see attractions in the park go away, but you can see why. It's great that (some rides have) no wait, but realize that means it's not very popular and it can probably be better used. I think sometimes fans aren't very objective when it comes to that. I'm not saying tear down all the classics. But to a certain degree, you do have to explain to the younger generation why some things are important, like the Tiki Room and Carousel of Progress."

Vaughn feels there are two sides to the issue, both of which get magnified on social media. She used Splash Mountain as an example. The attraction itself is one of the Disney Parks' premier rides, but the fact that was based on a racially charged movie like "Song of the South" necessitated a re-examination of its existence at some point. So, while it probably ultimately needed to be redone and she's glad "The Princess and the Frog" will be the new overlay, she gets that some people might have been able to separate the ride from its source: "I am for it just because I've always loved the Splash ride, but I always felt uncomfortable discussing it on my blog. That is the best water ride in the world ever, to me. I just wish it didn't come from where it came from. No matter what the change was, just convert it from 'Song of the South.' "

One need not discuss content with that level of controversy around it to get the trolls' blood boiling. Indeed, trying to engage with someone whose sole pleasure is derived from arguing with and angering a person on the internet they'll never actually meet (yes, it's as silly as it seems when you actually read it written out) is a poison apple that even Snow White would probably know to steer clear of. But when emotions are heightened, even online, disengaging can be tough, and it's only natural for everyone, every once in a while, to want to return fire.

"I have thrown my phone a few times. Then I told myself, 'OK, I've got to cope better,' " Wade said.

Steering clear of the negativity that could come from users decrying such things—or, honestly, pretty much anything that crosses users' minds—can be a part-time job in and of itself. Vaughn said the best strategy is to selectively engage: "If it's straight being mean and nothing constructive, I just block and delete." But listening to people who are honestly trying to help can be beneficial, such as one social media user who critiqued an early story she did about Halloween Horror Nights at Universal Studios. That person said her writing was decent but lacked depth and insight, and she used that to ultimately improve her product: "It's OK to make me better, make the blog better and help readers get the information they need."

Picking the right way to deliver that information on social media is also helpful. Hughley, for example, focuses first on Instagram and then Twitter, both because that's where her content is best-received and she wants to put her limited time to best use. Mongello, meanwhile, has created a veritable playbook on how to use Facebook but is more selective on other channels: "In 2020, you have to know where your audience is, where you can serve them best. Nobody wants to see me doing dances on TikTok."

Disney fans do, however, enjoy seeing visuals of all sorts from the parks. That's part of why Corless continued to adapt the WDW News Today social media feeds, featuring more photos on there and linking to even more pictures.

"We try to accommodate everyone," he said. "That's how you grow the business. As more people find us, we don't want to lose them."

Finding a way to push content while not operating a social media feed that's a pure commercial can be a tough thing to achieve. Mongello, who operates a Twitter handle under his own name as opposed to one under the WDW Radio name, pretty much sends out nothing but links to episodes. WDW News Today basically does likewise, while Disney Food Blog features a ton of pictures and click-baity captions. Roseboom shares a good amount of personal accounts from the parks and other areas of life, along with retweeting content from Attractions Magazine. Parrish does otherwise with the Thirty20Eight account, sometimes offering brief insight into a given episode he's sharing. Dizney Coast to Coast offers a mix of show and non-show fare, although all content has something to do with the company, whether it be notable anniversaries, old parks photos, user polls or Rick Moranis (and there's a lot of Rick Moranis).

While it doesn't take money to promote content on social media (assuming you're not crazy enough to pay for followers), there is still cost associated with using it.

"I think social media is important is important to grow your audience, but it is a super-time-consuming process," DePaoli said. "I personally kind of find it infuriating because I'd rather take the time and energy required to put into social media into producing a better podcast instead."

The key, he said, is for anyone using social media to promote their content to pick the platform that they like the most and that's most likely to reach their target audience. WDW Radio excels at live Facebook podcasts, for example, while Laughing Place funnels a lot of historical photos content on its Instagram feed to complement its news coverage. Of course, the help that larger operations are able to employ is a big benefit.

"It's impossible as a one-person business to do them all well at the same time. It's insanely time-consuming," DePaoli said.

Indeed, Hill said he's adapted over the years to incorporate social media into his regular routine—and it's an aspect of the job that many followers might not realize is structured like one would any other part of their job.

"We live in an age now where, look at how much info we get off of Twitter. A lot of people are spending a couple hours each morning on Twitter," he said. "You do the interview, you have the ingredients, you have your deadline. So much of this job today is, 'Did you put it on Instagram?' So much of this world is having the right skillset, but at the same time staying on top of the innovations that are going on."

But it's necessary, Frost contends, even as some creators still pine for simpler days. Despite taking to Twitter early on, Frost has since shifted the focus to his Facebook account, which generates more traffic for The Disney Blog now than his Twitter account despite its more nascent status. While figuring out the algorithms may never truly be possible, he's noticed that Facebook generates the most traffic early at night and later in the evening, including more international traffic that he would expect considering his site's admitted bias toward Walt Disney World.

Then, of course, there are the social media anomalies like a post he did on a baby porcupine born at Animal Kingdom in early 2020, which generated several times the normal impressions on his social media accounts. But by and large, he thinks he has social media figured out, for now: "What my readers want, based on talking to them, is they want to know the things that make the magic special."

Of course, capitalizing on trends can't hurt in the cause to get noticed. Wade did a two-part series for DisKingdom on the "Pokemon GO" locations at the Disney Parks in July 2016, when the mobile game was at the peak of its popularity. [1]

"That really took off," she said. "It was crazy. Everyone wanted to play then, even at the parks."

To further capitalize on a trend or breaking piece of news, repetition of content is a safe technique utilized by numerous content creators (because, show of hands, how many of you can remember even 25 percent of the posts you scrolled through while on the toilet yesterday?). That goes both for repeating the same post on different days and recycling content that becomes newly relevant. Mongello, for example, sometimes sends tweets promoting month- or even years-old episodes, something that is admittedly a lot easier for timeless productions like podcasts to do than straight news sites.

Keeping afloat in an ever-ebbing social media tide can be a challenge even for the most experiences users. Wolfe said the key to success for the Disney Food Blog feeds has been studying the landscape and ensuring best practices are adhered to as often as possible.

"The digital media space changes all the time, so we're constantly keeping an eye on trends and changes in how people want to consume media—as well as what questions they have. It's our goal to always provide the most credible, valuable, accessible content we possibly can, so that means making sure we're creating content that people can and want to consume. Throughout our experience we've seen social media develop, smartphones come into existence and food reviewing move from the domain of the few to the domain of the many. I think it's wonderful," she said.

Wade has followed a similar path. Her Instagram account, for example, was once simply pictures of Walt Disney World.

"As I evolved as a writer and actually wanted to narrow my focus, I overhauled it," she said. "I just focus now on travel and what you can do at Disney, what I do at Disney that I think people will like, and style."

That last element was a learned trait for Wade, who grew up not caring much about fashion. She only got into it a few years when she first heard about disneybounding: "I kind of dipped a toe in a bit, but I didn't really dive in. I saw friends doing it, and I thought, 'How can I do this myself?' I now go for a classic Hollywood style, incorporating a Disney character into it."

Vaughn has likewise treated the implementation of Instagram as a job requirement rather than leisure venture: "I'm not an Instagram person, but even when I go to Instagram and I know I'm taking a photo in front of the castle with these outfits, that's not me. I get done what I have to get done."

The #disneybound hashtag has, at any given moment, more than 1 million mentions on Instagram (the official @TheDisneyBound account has more than a quarter-million followers). And even for the most hardened heart, it would be nearly impossible not to smile at least at some of the photos, which could range from an Ariel-inspired skirt set being worn in a walk-in closet to a Minnie Mouse polka-dotted mask-and-tattoo combo worn mid-pandemic and a Skylar sisters pose ("Hamilton" counts as Disney now that it's been featured on Disney+) in front of Cinderella's Castle.

Disneybound style, like much content from all creators on social media, requires a good amount of attention to detail as well as imagination. And more and more people are dipping their toes into the water every month. Some are shamelessly trying to sell something. Others just wanna have fun. Still others are pushing some ulterior motive. But for whatever reason, more users migrate online weekly. That makes the struggle to get noticed real, to be sure. And it can create aggravations for consumer and creator alike.

"I make sure to take time for myself," Wade replied when asked how she handles the negativity that can be found (or that finds her). "Sometimes your body is giving you signs, and you ignore them. If you feel overwhelmed, take an hour or two to watch Netflix."

Some creators can find time to chill scarce, though, when it's so easy to drown in the sea that is 21st century social media. An hour or two examining hashtags will find millions of posts relating to #DisneyLove, #DisneyChannel (although who's still watching cable is a mystery), #DisneyAddict, #DisneyCosplay, #DisneyChristmas (which somehow still has more than half a million mentions in mid-July), #DisneyVillains and several reveling in that fact that Disney fandom somehow equates one to being a geek or nerd—in the most affectionate way possible—including #DisneyGeek and #Disblerd (Disney Black Nerd). For every hashtag, there are dozens if not hundreds of accounts devoted to those and ancillary topics. And more will rush into the mainstream between the time these words first hit the page and you consume them.

And, like the light at the end of a sewage-filled tunnel, creators worldwide will dive into them in pursuit of the glory on the other side.

"Fragmentation was going to happen anyway. The fight to remain relevant is diversifying," Yaglenski said. "All we can do is we keep content relevant."

Source:

1. https://diskingdom.com/2016/07/12/gotta-catch-em-disney-parks/

CHAPTER THIRTEEN

Believing All the Way, Implicitly and Unquestionably

To wrap things up, every content creator who was interviewed for this book was asked two simple questions: What was the biggest hit at one of the Disney Parks since 2000, and what was the biggest miss?

- Brown feels blue about the loss of the Maelstrom, which was removed from Sweden in Epcot's World Showcase in favor of Frozen Ever After in 2016. "I think that kind of opened the door at Disney that can't be really be shut now," said Brown, referencing the introduction of intellectual properties into Epcot—which was established as an IP-free entity meant to inspire creativity and foresight. "It's not the same feeling now. It's more family-friendly now, which is weird." Brown feels improvements at Animal Kingdom are much more praise-worthy. He said expanded shows and entertainment, such as the since-shuttered Rivers of Light show that was introduced in 2017 when the park established nighttime hours, make for a much more fulfilling experience. "It's just a different experience at night," he said. Brown also praised the "Avatar"-inspired land of Pandora, which opened in 2017 and deserves a lot of credit for inspiring the enveloping environment that is Star Wars: Galaxy's Edge.

- Burbank's biggest hit is Walt Disney Studios Park at Disneyland Paris. "Watching 'The Imagineering Story' explains why it was built. Being a Disney fan, you start to hear things and you get them in your head," he said, alluding to the flack Disney's French entry has gotten over the years. His biggest miss was the original version of Disney's California Adventure, which has largely been regarded as the biggest mistake at any park at any time period. [1] Although Burbank feels even the worst parks have something to enjoy, "it's just so clear that (California Adventure) was not a great idea, and they had this idea, 'Let's just throw this over here and piece it together.'" While not as bad as that, Universal Studios has gotten too much credit in his opinion. "(The Wizarding World of) Harry Potter is great, but when you look at what else they've done, it's not a great track record. Just variations of the same ride system. Transformers (The Ride-3D), (Race Through New York Starring) Jimmy Fallon, (The Amazing Adventures of) Spider-Man—you know what emotion it's going to evoke. You'll know all the beats. I don't think Universal is pushing for Disney's crown as much as some people think it is."
- Corless is more or less bored with most of the park additions of the past two years, feeling that the company is resting on its laurels a bit and not innovating in the same way as decades ago, during which attractions like Wonders of Life and Journey into Imagination made impressions that have never left those who got to experience them. "Rise of the Resistance is great, but I'm not

floored with (the new features) otherwise. Pixar Pier and Toy Story Land, those are the hallmark of the current environment. They don't feel like Disney to me. They feel cheap and easy and quick. Imagineers were designing everything in Florida with interior queues. And then in 2018, it just like, 'Outdoor roller coaster, no shade—it's fine.' Waiting to ride Slinky Dog Dash, we would see 40 people under a single patio umbrella. This is not what you could do. You did not think of guest comfort." That extends to Star Wars: Galaxy's Edge, which Corless called passable but nowhere near what it could be. "I think they picked something that doesn't connect with people. You've got to watch the cartoons and read comics (to get all the references). If you're that person, you go there and you have a wonderful time. My mom looked around and said she was disappointed: 'I didn't expect this. I don't know what, but I thought it would be something else.' There's no water, no moving elements. Very few things make you feel like it's a living, breathing place. I think Lucasfilm is too nerdy for their own good. People are willing to go on a ride that's completely original. But when you have something that everybody has an idea about, there are things that people expect. Tony Baxter would always tell us, 'Don't do the short version of the movie,' but that's what people expect. The guest already has a preconceived notion of what this is. There are certain moments from the film that people expect to be there. If you haven't read those novels, you going into Docking Bay 7 and you feel like you're just sitting in a warehouse. I have seen these movies 100 times, and I have no idea what's going on." As far as hits, Corless was impressed with Cars Land, a version of Radiator Springs from the "Cars" franchise that went into California Adventure as part of that park's revamp in 2012. "That park was kind of a dump, and it made it instead a place in California that people wanted to go. I never feel the same way about anything else new that I still feel about Cars Land. Now, that's the first place I want to go before I land. There's just something very reassuring. It's homey, lots of good attractions. It's an inviting place to spend time."

- DePaoli feels that stagnation on a large scale in Florida has been Disney's biggest mistake. "The biggest misstep is not having a new park at Walt Disney World in the 21st century ... it's been 22 years now without a new park at Walt Disney World, which I consider to be the home base for Disney theme parks. It's still mind-blowing to me that we don't have fifth gate there ... Billions have been dumped into the parks to fix them, but to not have a new gate—and the amount of land they have (about 25,000 acres, half of which has been used [2]). It's crazy to me. Building a new 'Star Wars' land is not building a new theme park." Universal Studios Orlando will have a third gate in 2023 when Epic Universe opens (along with the Volcano Bay water park), putting it only one behind Disney. "That is a really bad thing happening that I think (Chapek) is going to have to deal with, and I think he'll have to quickly." Disney's expansion in California, for as much criticism as it's drawn, should still be lauded by fans, DePaoli said. "The addition of Disney's California Adventure and Downtown Disney in the 21st century made Disneyland a resort. Before 2001, it was a day trip to

Disneyland. At the beginning of 2001, regardless of how successful Disney's California Adventure was, it became a resort." A huge Halloween fan, he's also enthused about the earlier advent of the parks' haunted events, which now come before most children have even gone back to school for the fall: "The more we can celebrate, the better."

- Duffy is done with the wave of IPs making their way into the parks. He'd much rather see original attractions than reworked rides based on *Guardians of the Galaxy* (one of each will exist in both domestic Disney Parks before long), *Moana* and other existing properties. "I understand why, but what was the last original idea in the parks? Probably Mystic Manor in 2013 in Shanghai. Before that, it was Soarin' (in 2001). No original ideas get to come out anymore." But advancements in technology have made up for that, allowing attractions that may be based on existing characters to at least still provide some thrills. "The tech has changed so much that it does enhance the experience. There's so much more that's going to happen."
- Frost has a three-pronged fork of issues with the parks. He is no fan of the evolution of the FastPass and Disney Dining initiatives as this century has progressed. "I get the idea that Disney is going to make more money because of there being no lines, but I think that the way it exists really takes a lot of the fun and the spontaneity out of the parks," he said, lamenting the need to plan months in advance both for what to ride and where and when to eat. He was more blunt when it comes to eating: "The Disney Dining program has destroyed the dining experience at the parks. There has been

some recovery recently, but for a long time the price went up and the quality and selection went down." He also decried the inability of locals or those staying off-property to take part in the programs: "The ability to get reservations without a resort stay is little to none." Both of these initiatives point to a desire for more revenue, something Frost thinks extends to its emphasis on the Disney Vacation Club (which, even if you've gotten roped into one of those presentations at the kiosks every 500 feet throughout the parks, might not totally make sense unless you vacation with your calculus professor). A focus on that, he said, gives Disney a desired consistent revenue stream but comes at the expense of the majority of the park guests: "Because they're able to do that, they've cut back on a lot of the services they were able to do. They're able to get away with the same thing year after year. They know the core audience will be returning because they are under contract. That meant for a long time, Walt Disney World was not adding capacity. Things were pretty flat for a long time." That's a more infuriating notion, Frost said, when you consider how well the company can perform when it exerts effort. Recent expansions like Fantasyland and Pandora did not disappoint, he said, and Galaxy's Edge—specifically Rise of the Resistance—represent the pinnacle of what Disney can do, at least domestically: "It has its flaws, but it's the most immersive land, and it's transforming the idea of what a theme park is and can be." He also mentioned Tokyo DisneySea as a masterpiece, based on pictures and videos, but without having made a personal visit he could not put it atop his list.

- Heaton said the complexity of what a trip to Walt Disney World has become is the biggest misstep this century. Guests now pretty basically have to decide 60-180 days before they arrive where and when they will eat, and what attractions they'll start each day with—and if they wait until 59 days before there's a good chance they'll have to settle for a fourth or fifth option. "There are benefits to Magic Bands and FastPass, like not having to get up so early (to be first in line). But with people who are not as die-hard, a lot of the changes, in Florida especially, have made it harder on the average guest. The idea of being a kid and waiting in lines as a kid—yes, it was hot. Yes, it was crowded. But it was simple. There are so many things that have gotten so complicated, like virtual queues for Rise of the Resistance. For every change, there is a benefit. However, I feel like even then there's a risk to having so many hurdles to overcome. For somebody who goes on their first trip and is spending that much money, there are decisions that make it a lot harder than it could be ... Going to a theme park should not be that complicated." Less complicated are the improvements Heaton said Disney has made to Animal Kingdom to make it simultaneously feel more like a Disney park yet retain a distinct feel. "What they've done to make the Animal Kingdom such a comfortable place to hang out and so unique," he said. "They put in characters in some interesting ways. It seems to have somehow avoided some of the pitfalls of some of the other parks. They've found ways to make it even better."
- Hill also considers how Walt Disney World is visited to be the biggest mountain guests have

to climb—a mountain so large that many people are willing to pay Testa, Hill's blog partner, to get park optimization plans and be able to do more during their visits. And the other associated costs, according to Hill, make that a mountain that may not be worth climbing before too long. "You used to walk through the park and think, 'What am I going to do?' You wandered. You discovered the different things ... I miss when you could be spontaneous and fun. Every year, it seems to be that much more expensive to spend time there. I worry that Disney is becoming like pro sports. There's going to come a time when there's going to be a ceiling on what people are willing to pay." But while guests and their complex schedules are a miss, Hill feels the consistency the parks have improved upon this century is a hit. "The architecture of reassurance ... why we go to Disney theme parks. There's always going to be a parade at 3, fireworks at 9. Everything there is reassuring."

- Holley is another content creator who's fed up with the lack of original content created at the parks. "It started with putting Nemo in The Living Seas (in 2006). Seabase Alpha was such an original experience. Nemo fits, but it's kind of that slippery slope." That being said, any improvements to Epcot are needed, and Holley is jolly about the attention coming to Walt Disney's World second gate—including a space-themed restaurant, a ride based on "Ratatouille" and a reimagining of the park's lands. [3] "It's sorely needed. That's going to be the biggest upside."
- Hughley has suffered more sticker shock with every trip to the parks: "Yes, prices going up is nothing new and will continue to do so. (But)

the Disney Parks are turning into a once-in-a-lifetime event for some families." What guest are paying for is of high quality, though, in her eyes: "I have enjoyed the additions of Toy Story Land and Galaxy's Edge. I am looking forward to seeing how 'The Princess and the Frog' will be incorporated into an attraction. Change can be hard, but (it's) needed and welcomed to me."

- Mongello showed off the breadth of his Disney knowledge by citing as his biggest miss Stitch's Supersonic Celebration (go ahead, Google it. I'll wait). The show lasted less than two months in Tomorrowland in spring 2009. He cautioned, though, that even a nearly universally panned idea like that one has fans somewhere: "I'm sure that some kid out there thought that was the best thing he or she saw." For the biggest hit, Mongello didn't mention an attraction or land but a person: "Bob Iger is the biggest hit. His legacy—history will look back fondly upon him. The growth and acquisitions he made with this company—he led unprecedented growth. There's a lot of Walt in Bob Iger in terms of philosophy, surrounding yourself with people who are the very best at what they do. What he's been able to do has been remarkable." Not directly involved with the parks, Mongello also cited the success of his Dream Team Project, which has raised more than $350,000 to date to help send sick children to Walt Disney World through the Make-a-Wish Foundation of America.
- Parrish echoes the sentiment of many Disneyphiles in decrying the fact that The Great Movie Ride had to perish. "To think that we had to lose that signature attraction to get this new attraction—people won't be upset with Mickey

& Minnie's Runaway Railway. It just didn't need to replace that. That's like removing Spaceship Earth. And (Hollywood Studios) is a park that's thirsty for attractions. You didn't remove Star Tours when you put in Galaxy's Edge." And Disney's ability to realize its early mistakes with California Adventure tops Parrish's hit list. "It was flawed from the start. And 100 percent of that was budget cuts. It seemed like that had really fleshed out ideas and were told they can't use those. By 2007, they decided to invest billions in redoing it. If you're going to have a park next to Disneyland, it should at least be a warranted No. 2 gate."

- Roseboom ventured off-property in identifying his biggest miss, Fast & Furious: Supercharged at Universal Studios. "It's just kind of a disappointment what they did with it and they could have done with it," he said. But some of the advanced technology used on that and other rides was considered by Roseboom to be the biggest hit. He cited the projections cast on Cinderella's Castle and the screens on Mickey & Minnie's Runaway Railway as changing the game. Another major leap was Wizarding World, which he said forced Disney to step its game up in terms of land creation and immersion. "It sets the theme parks in a new world with detail. That was the new bar to reach, and I think Disney has reached it and perhaps surpassed it with Star Wars: Galaxy's Edge," he said.
- Vaughn is not impressed with what Hollywood Studios has become, when considered from a 199-foot view: "The overall vibe has been kind of underwhelming. They just kind of started putting things in there. It's a theme

park where you don't know where it stands. I don't know what to describe it as ... I don't know what the messaging has been since the start of the century, and I don't know exactly where they're going with it." Within Hollywood Studios, though, she's thrilled with Rise of the Resistance, if not all of Galaxy's Edge: "I can't say anything bad about that ride. It's incredible."

- Wade was ready to let Disney's 24-hour events sink by the time she was through with them. What started off as truly special events with special theming and attractions ended up with Disney putting forth no more effort that allowing people to stay for a day straight, she said: "The first one had special characters, parties—there was a lot more going on and a lot more excitement ... It was fun versus the last one, where there were no special characters. There was nothing special about it." The parks had a huge hit, in her eyes, in New Fantasyland, which opened in 2012 while Wade was taking part in the Disney College Program at Walt Disney World: "It was very well done. It was nice to be part of a big moment in Disney history." She also had high marks for the newest incarnation of Mickey's Royal Friendship Faire, which was the first time the show featured a Black princess (Tiana).
- Wolfe was unable to pinpoint one miss at the parks (although, if you read through enough of her site's reviews, you'll come upon some individual dishes she was willing to pass on). "Disney is always changing, and while some of our favorite experiences and restaurants will be replaced, there's always something new to experience and enjoy." Not surprisingly, she was quick to cite the evolution of the food scene at the parks as the

biggest hit. She considers that an evolutionary must during a time when 80 percent or more of park-goers can instantly put a meal on blast with the miniature computer in their pocket. "I think the food scene at the parks has taken a huge step forward since smartphones and social media became a thing. Once Disney discovered that the food was a destination, they started putting more thought and effort into it."

- Yaglenski reached just past the time limit given, citing the January 1999 closure of Horizons at Epcot as the parks' biggest miss. "It was the best ride Disney ever produced. It was the extension of the Carousel of Progress into the future. It did so well on so many levels what Disney was all about," he said. Yaglenski's biggest hit was simultaneously one of its biggest misses—the hiring of Michael Eisner as Disney chairman and CEO, a post he held from 1984-2005. Under his watch, Disney's animation and theme park operations were revitalized, although by the turn of the century the company had grown stale enough under his watch to cause mass creator and investor defections. [4] "He did more for the organization, but he gets trampled in Disney lore now. Early on, him and (late Disney president) Frank Wells were probably the best thing to happen to the parks in a long time. He ended up staying too long. In the context of everything, a lot of what we have today, we have him to thank for bringing it back to life. He fixed a lot of problems and saved the company ... the parks were almost broken up and sold for pieces."

Sources:

1. https://www.themeparktourist.com/features/20151212/31106/california-mis-adventure-how-disneylands-second-gate-crashed-burned-and-was
2. https://wdwnews.com/fact-sheets/2014/10/31/walt-disney-world-fun-facts
3. https://web.archive.org/web/20190827064110/https://disneyparks.disney.go.com/blog/2019/08/new-details-revealed-for-the-historic-transformation-of-epcot-underway-at-walt-disney-world-resort
4. https://usatoday30.usatoday.com/money/media/2003-12-01-disney-words_x.htm

CHAPTER FOURTEEN

Nobody Gets Forgotten

For more on the content creators featured in this book, here's how you can check out their work:

- attractionsmagazine.com; @ AttractionsMagazine on Facebook and Instagram; @Attractions on Twitter
- disneyfoodblog.com; @DisneyFoodBlog on Facebook, Instagram and Twitter
- disthrubrowneyes.com; @DizThruBrownEyes on Instagram; @DizThruBrwnEyes on Twitter
- dizneycoasttocoast.com; @DizneyCTC on Facebook, Twitter and Instagram
- enchantedtikitalk.com; @EnchantedTikiTalk on Facebook; @TikiTalkPodcast on Instagram and Twitter
- intercot.com; @Intercot on Facebook, Twitter and Instagram
- jimhillmedia.com; @JimHillMediaNews on Facebook; @JimHillMedia on Instagram and Twitter
- nateparrish.libsyn.com; @WEDwayradio on Facebook and Twitter; @NateParrishStuff on Instagram
- teawithv.squarespace.com; @ hecallsmepineapple-princess on Instagram; @hecallsmePP on Twitter

- thedisneyblog.com; @TheDisneyBlog Facebook, Instagram and Twitter
- themeparkhipster.com; @ThemeParkHipster on Facebook and Instagram; @ThemeParkHipste on Twitter
- thirty20eight.libsyn.com; @Thirty20Eight on Instagram and Twitter
- tomorrowsociety.com; @tomorrowsociety on Facebook and Instagram; @tomorrowsoc on Twitter
- wdwnewstoday.com; @WDWNT on Facebook, Twitter and Instagram
- wdwradio.com; @WDWRadio on Facebook; @ LouMongello on Instagram and Twitter

About the Author

Paul Lane has been a professional writer since receiving a newspaper journalism degree from Syracuse University in 2000 (great timing). His work has been featured in the *Buffalo News*, *American City Business Journals* and the *New York Times*.

His love of Disney stems from a high school band trip in 1996 that allowed him to play trumpet in Epcot and sparked a life-long love.

The Buffalo native now lives in nearby Niagara Falls (the American side) with his wife, daughter and son, all of whom have been infected by his Disney bug. He is also a proud #BillsMafia member.

Find him on Twitter @AuthorPaulLane or write to needsmespinach@yahoo.com.

About Theme Park Press

Theme Park Press publishes books primarily about the Disney company, its history, culture, films, animation, and theme parks, as well as theme parks in general.

Our authors include noted historians, animators, Imagineers, and experts in the theme park industry.

We also publish many books by first-time authors, with topics ranging from fiction to theme park guides.

And we're always looking for new talent. If you'd like to write for us, or if you're interested in the many other titles in our catalog, please visit:

www.ThemeParkPress.com

Theme Park Press Newsletter

Subscribe to our free email newsletter and enjoy:

- Free book downloads and giveaways
- Access to excerpts from our many books
- Announcements of forthcoming releases
- Exclusive additional content and chapters
- And more good stuff available nowhere else

To subscribe, visit www.ThemeParkPress.com, or send email to newsletter@themeparkpress.com.

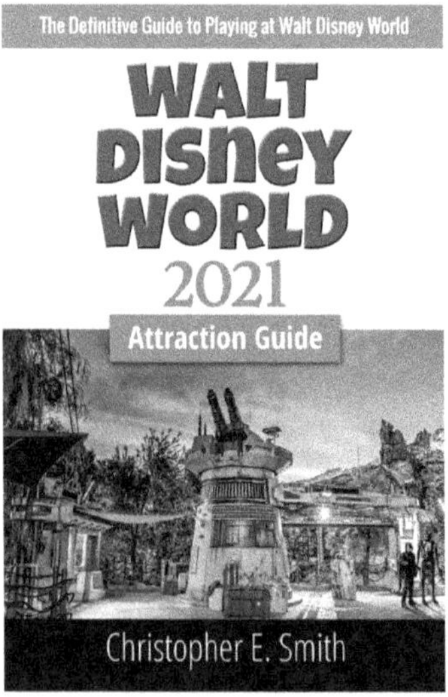

Read more about these books
and our many other titles at:

www.ThemeParkPress.com

www.ingramcontent.com/pod-product-compliance
Lightning Source LLC
LaVergne TN
LVHW022044200926
848481LV00003B/789